LEADERSHIP
MASTERY

Shippensburg, PA

**Other Harrison House titles
by Billy Epperhart**

Money Mastery

Change Mastery

LEADERSHIP
MASTERY

GROWING
YOUR CAPACITY
TO LEAD YOURSELF,
OTHERS, AND YOUR
ORGANIZATION

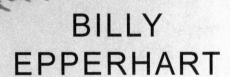

BILLY
EPPERHART

DEDICATION

To all the great people over the past forty years I've enjoyed serving in ministry and business. It's been a privilege.

To my wife, Becky, who has stood beside me for the past forty-five years. Our best years are just ahead.

To Andrew Wommack for the honor of serving at Andrew Wommack Ministries and Charis Bible College. My heartfelt thanks. It's been a divine connection.

Disclaimer: This book contains information that is intended to help the readers be better informed in dealing with change and the challenges it brings to life. It is presented as general advice using the author's experience and best judgment but is in no way to be considered a substitute for necessary care provided by a physician or other medical professional.

Published by Harrison House Publishers

Shippensburg, PA 17257

Cover design by: Eileen Rockwell

ISBN 13 TP: 978-1-6803-1421-2

ISBN 13 eBook: 978-1-6803-1422-9

ISBN 13 HC: 978-1-6803-1440-3

ISBN 13 LP: 978-1-6803-1439-7

For Worldwide Distribution, Printed in the U.S.A.

2 3 4 5 6 7 8 / 24 23 22 21 20

CONTENTS

FOREWORD

I've known about Billy Epperhart for decades, even back when he was a pastor. But it's only in the last six years that I've really got to know him as he first became a vital part of our Business school in Charis Bible College and then a vital part of my leadership team for Andrew Wommack Ministries. He was indispensable in our negotiations to acquire a $21 million, 336 tract of land with a 60,000 sq. ft. building on it. He has also been vitally involved in all aspects of our administration. He directed our transition from a simple 501 (c) 3 to five different corporations which include holding companies and for profit and political companies. He has dealt directly with our auditors and all aspects of running a $70 million ministry. He has personally mentored all of our top management and I've seen them grow tremendously under his leadership.

Billy has also represented me overseas in numerous locations and started micro finance banks which are very successful. As my personal envoy, he has handled problems which have arisen in a number of our foreign offices and I've been very pleased with the results. Billy is a team player and not out to promote himself. That's a rare quality which has led me to put a huge amount of trust in him and his abilities.

I'm honored to recommend Billy as a person and his ministry on leadership. I've seen it up close and personal and know that anyone, at any level can benefit from his teaching on leadership.

—Andrew Wommack
Founder and President of
Andrew Wommack Ministries and Charis Bible College.

INTRODUCTION

Every one of us will in some way or another be placed in at least small positions of leadership throughout our lives. In fact, leadership is a nuanced subject, and it filters throughout every facet of our lives.

Some people choose—or are thrust into—large leadership roles, while others assume smaller leadership roles in a myriad of life settings. Some are born with innate leadership skills while others must strive to develop the skillset. No matter—this book holds lessons for every type of leader. Whether you want to rise in the corporate ranks, jumpstart your own business, pioneer a church or volunteer at a nonprofit, become a better parent or grandparent, or you're a college student on the edge of the rest of your life, this book will guide you to bigger and better things.

Let's face it, all leadership is not created equal. That's why *Leadership Mastery* is about good leadership on its way to great leadership. It's about preparing yourself in small ways and big ways. It's about instilling in yourself a spirit of faith and the ability to communicate your vision to others. It's about recognizing that great leaders are made from the inside out. That's why I wrote *Leadership Mastery* in three parts: Leadership and You; Leadership and Others; and Leadership and Your Organization.

Leadership and You

Great leadership starts with a great leader. And being a great leader starts with preparing yourself through personal development, so we begin here. You will learn how to overcome obstacles of disappointment while growing and changing through courage and faith.

A great leader is also one who knows his or her purpose, and a shared purpose unites people. You cannot lead your family or your organization without a destination in mind. Otherwise, you'll be wandering in the dark! In Part One of *Leadership Mastery* we look at how to find or refine your purpose and establish a pattern for success.

Leadership and Others

In Part Two of *Leadership Mastery*, we focus outward and consider others. Whether as a parent, older sibling, CEO, or a pastor, leadership starts in the home. Leadership of a family is a representation of what leaders of organizations need to do. Leadership is not isolated to your business. You cannot spend all your energy trying to be a good business or church leader but neglect your family.

Over the years, I realized exactly how large and problematic the emotional disconnect is that we suffer from in this country. Parents—fathers especially—have too often neglected to get emotionally involved with their kids. One of the most important things you can do as a parent is to make sure you are in a loving relationship with your spouse and emotionally connecting with your teenagers. In fact, there must be a spiritual and emotional bond between you and your children. Don't stick your head in the sand and fail to recognize the influences attacking them from every peer culture and social media forefront in this day and age.

In Part Two, we also focus on how to lead others through prayer and discipleship and how leaders can deal with criticism from others.

Leadership and Your Organization

The third part of *Leadership Mastery* is probably the reason you picked up this book. This is the part where I teach you how to lead your church, your business, or your organization through systems and procedures.

I started my career as a pastor and since then I have founded and owned several businesses, learning a lot about leadership along the way. Today I am the co-CEO and Executive Vice President of Andrew Wommack Ministries, which employees more than 600 people. I am also the founder of two nonprofit organizations: WealthBuilders and Tricord Global. I share that knowledge with you in the chapters that follow. This third part of the book is a tad more technical, and we will talk about report forms, job descriptions, and various other organizational do's and don'ts.

There's an old axiom that says, "You can lead a horse to water, but you can't force it to drink." I have found that rings true of people as well. Being a good leader isn't just about knowing how to motivate your employees, it's about giving them the tools or action steps they need to get to where they want to be. Can you delegate and provide direction?

To lead an organization effectively, I have discovered you have to be both a leader and a manager. It is essential that you can motivate and be personable with your employees. It is also essential that you are enforcing systems and procedures that will help your organization thrive.

In the final part of *Leadership Mastery*, I teach you how to be a leader-manager hybrid so that your organization and your people can not only thrive but excel.

PART ONE

LEADERSHIP AND YOU

Back in 1999 and 2000, I was navigating unexpected territory with the rest of my community as we reeled from the Columbine High School massacre where two teens went on a shooting spree that killed thirteen people and wounded more than twenty others before committing suicide. As a pastor who presided over four of the funerals, I found myself thrust into the media forefront. I remember being taken aback by the reaction of some of the national television anchors during their reporting of the Columbine tragedy. One interaction particularly stands out to me.

An anchorman was interviewing me when, during a break between segments, he began to cry. Through his tears, he said, "Pastor, will you pray for me?"

"Sure, I'll pray for you," I said. "What would you like prayer for?"

"Pastor, I'm scared right now. I know I haven't been the father I need to be. When you were talking about that on the air a minute ago, it just hit me right in the heart. I need you to pray for me."

This was not the only conversation I had like that. I began to see exactly how large and problematic the emotional disconnect is that we suffer from in this country. Parents—fathers especially—have neglected getting emotionally involved with their children. One of the most important things you can do as a parent is to make sure that you are in a loving relationship with your spouse and that you are emotionally connecting with your teenagers. There must be a spiritual and emotional bond between you and your children. We cannot stick our heads in the sand! Instead, we must recognize the influences that are attacking our children in unprecedented ways.

But you did not pick up a book on parenting, so why am I talking about it? As mentioned in the Introduction, leadership is a nuanced subject. It's not isolated to your business. Leadership begins with you and ends with you—rippling outward to and from everything connected to you. That's the difference between someone who leads and someone who is a leader. It's oftentimes the difference between success and failure because it speaks to character and wisdom.

There is no shortage of knowledge in this day and age. It's only one Google, one college degree, one new hire, or one consultant away. But true leadership requires a leader with the wisdom to guide the knowledge and the character to handle it with integrity. Being a good leader is also about living in a state of preparation for bigger and better things. It's about instilling in yourself a spirit of faith and the ability to communicate your vision to others. And it's about cultivating the favor of God.

The Favor Factor

It's important for you to understand God's favor—what it is and who receives it. Favor makes all the difference in doing business, leading ministry, and building an organization. What is favor? It's God's grace and approval. One person called it tangible evidence of God's approval (see Isaiah 66:2; 2 Chronicles 16:9). Who receives this favor? A leader who is actively learning to be a better leader or who is in a state of preparation. Why? Because favor is attracted to a spirit of preparation.

Let's look at this principle in Matthew 25:14-29:

> *"For the kingdom of heaven is like a man traveling to a far country, who called his own servants and delivered his goods to them. And to one he gave five talents, to another two, and to another one, to each according to his own ability; and immediately he went on a journey. Then he who had received the five talents went and traded with them, and made another five talents. And likewise he who had received two gained two more also. But he who had received one went and dug in the ground, and hid his lord's money. After a long time the lord of those servants came and settled accounts with them.*
>
> *"So he who had received five talents came and brought five other talents, saying, 'Lord, you delivered to me five talents; look, I have gained five more talents besides them.' His lord said to him, 'Well done, good and faithful servant; you were faithful over a few things, I will make you ruler over many things. Enter into the joy of your lord.' He also who had received two talents came and said, 'Lord, you delivered to me two talents; look, I have gained two more talents besides them.' His lord said to him, 'Well done, good and faithful servant; you have been faithful over a few things, I will make you ruler over many things. Enter into the joy of your lord.'*
>
> *"Then he who had received the one talent came and said, 'Lord, I knew you to be a hard man, reaping where you have not sown, and gathering where you have not scattered*

seed. And I was afraid, and went and hid your talent in the ground. Look, there you have what is yours.'

"But his lord answered and said to him, 'You wicked and lazy servant, you knew that I reap where I have not sown, and gather where I have not scattered seed. So you ought to have deposited my money with the bankers, and at my coming I would have received back my own with interest. So take the talent from him, and give it to him who has ten talents. For to everyone who has, more will be given, and he will have abundance; but from him who does not have, even what he has will be taken away.'"

The first question that comes to my mind when reading this passage, is why did one person get five talents, one get two, and one get one? Was God, or the master, being choosy? The answer is yes—in the sense that he already had recognized those servants. He watched their work and measured their abilities. So when the master looked at the first servant, he saw someone whom he believed could handle five talents. He thought the same with the second servant.

I don't know this for sure, but I think he looked at the last servant and thought, *I'm going to take a chance on this guy.* Maybe up to this point the servant had done little to be recognized for or tallied to his credit.

The second interesting thing that happens is that the master takes one talent away from the last servant. But he goes beyond that! He gives that one talent to the servant who had been entrusted with five. That servant now has eleven talents.

The question that jumps out at me is why did the master choose this servant? The answer was already mentioned earlier: favor is attracted to preparation. This principle is clearly illustrated here. I would guess that the one who was given five talents had been preparing for this moment for years. He didn't know what the moment would look like exactly, but he showed up and diligently did the work and bettered himself. He proved himself worthy of an investment, day by day. When it came down to it, there was something about him that stood out to the master. It's safe to say that the one who was given two talents had done some preparation, too. The last servant simply had not been preparing for the moment of opportunity.

So, why did the first servant get that one extra talent? The first two servants both did the same in doubling what they were given, so why the first and not the second? What did the first do exactly to earn it? The answer is nothing. It was pure favor of the master—the kind of favor that gets showered on top of a spirit of preparation.

There's another Bible account I read several years ago that taught me more about this idea of favor. It's from 2 Kings 25:27-30 and Jeremiah 52:31-33:

> *Now it came to pass in the thirty-seventh year of the captivity of Jehoiachin king of Judah, in the twelfth month, on the twenty-seventh day of the month, that Evil-Merodach king of Babylon, in the year that he began to reign, released Jehoiachin king of Judah from prison. He spoke kindly to him, and gave him a more prominent seat than those of the kings who were with him in Babylon. So Jehoiachin changed from his prison garments, and he ate bread regularly before the king all the days of his life. And as for his provisions, there was a regular ration given him by the king, a portion for each day, all the days of his life.*

Jehoiachin was a king in captivity to another king. In fact, he was one of several kings in captivity to the king of Babylon. One day, seemingly at random, the king of Babylon reached down and pulls Jehoiachin up above the other kings. He takes him out of prison, gives him a daily allowance, a new set of clothes, and lets him eat at his table every day.

When I first read this, I wondered why. Why did the king suddenly choose to favor Jehoiachin? I did a little digging and found out that the name Jehoiachin literally means *preparation*. Jehoiachin was in captivity for thirty-seven years; but obviously, he did not sit by idly letting his life waste away. I think he was preparing for all those years—actively bettering himself in some way. And the king of Babylon noticed!

We can learn a lot from both of these men—the servant given five talents and Jehoiachin. Favor is attracted to a spirit of preparation. That's why you are reading this book right now. It's why you are a reader and a learner. You too, even now, are preparing yourself. So, get your antennas up and yours eyes and ears open, because favor is coming to your life.

Finding Your Purpose

Many years ago, I heard a minister say that everyone goes through three primary phases of life:

1. **Discovery phase:** You actively learn who you are and where you fit.

2. **Productive phase:** You become incredibly productive living out of who you are. It's a stage of lots of accomplishment.

3. **Wisdom phase:** You desire to give back and pour into other people. You have learned through experience and want to share what you know.

Romans 12:2 says, "*And do not be conformed to this world, but be transformed by the renewing of your mind, that you may prove what is that good and acceptable and perfect will of God.*" Notice that there is a good will of God and an acceptable will of God—and we should desire to be in the perfect will of God. The good news is that you can be in God's perfect will at each stage of life. This is true even though each phase may look different as you grow, mature, and change, and as people come and go in your life. The key is to stay rooted in your God-given purpose no matter how many things around you change.

Drawing from the Inside

Proverbs 20:5 (NIV) reads, "*The purposes of a person's heart are deep waters, but one who has insight draws them out.*" To better understand what that means to us today, let me use a fly-fishing analogy. When I go fly-fishing on the rivers of Colorado, I like to use a wet fly. It goes underwater, but I have an indicator on top. The biggest fish are in the deepest waters, so that's really where I want to place my lure. When I'm fishing, I need to get the nymph down where the fish are feeding. Once I get a hit, I begin to draw out that fish.

The purposes of God are the same way. They're not going to come from listening to all the surface noise around you—social media, print media, television, friends, or people in general. There are a lot of voices and noise in this world, but the real purposes of God are in your heart. A person of understanding will draw them out.

How do you draw out God's purposes from your heart?

1. Get alone with God, get quiet, and pray. Ask the Holy Spirit to reveal your purpose to you and then listen to what He tells you to do. As you begin to pray this way and tune out the other voices, the purposes of God will become clearer. It won't happen in one five-minute

quiet time. You need to practice waiting in His presence and prepare your heart for it. Read the Scriptures and ask God to open your eyes and ears to hear what He's saying to you. Certain things will be highlighted and seem good to you. When that happens, follow that revelation God is giving you.

2. The next step is to listen for verification from others. As you begin to put into practice what God has revealed to you and take steps in your purpose, other people will notice and confirm for you that they recognize it. This may be as simple as someone saying, "Hey, you're really good at that!" Treasure those moments. God is speaking through them.

3. Last, watch for fruit. You will see that fruit results from your efforts, although maybe not immediately and maybe not in the most expected way. But fruit will confirm that you are following the purposes of God.

Getting over Fear

What do you do if you have a dream in your heart and a purpose God has outlined for you, but you're afraid to make the jump? Second Timothy 1:7 has the answer: *"God has not given us a spirit of fear, but of power and of love and of a sound mind."* Here's how to live that out:

1. Never make a decision out of fear. There are two sides to this instruction: don't pro-actively make a decision out of fear and don't *not* make a decision out of fear. In other words, take time to analyze your fear in prayer. Ask the Holy Spirit to give you a spirit of power, of

love, and of a sound mind. It's important to learn how to distinguish your own fears from the Holy Spirit's stop sign. Do not give your fears more merit than they deserve.

2. Take a step toward your dream. One of the mentors in my life would always say, "Go touch your dream." In those days, he was talking about something physical or material, like a certain kind of car or house. He would encourage me to go and physically touch those things that I wanted. It's still good advice today as long as you're not obsessed with material dreams. Remember that real dreams and real purpose are much deeper than material things.

what is my purpose? 2 chars?

I once heard of a program that let people try a career for two to six weeks. You could shadow a radio disc jockey for that time period, asking questions and basically trying on the job for size. It gave people a chance to touch their dream without leaving everything behind.

There's a reason this method is helpful. It allows you to overcome fear by taking action. Taking action toward your dream or purpose moves you beyond fear, and it works one small step at a time.

When I wanted to start the nonprofit Tricord Global, providing microcredit or small loans to the poor in developing nations, the first action I had to take was to actually establish it. It took me two years to finally get all of the approvals squared away before I could proceed with our first investment. I remember that first time clearly. We were in Africa, and I felt in over my head. There was a lot of fear in that moment. *What if we fail?* I continually wondered. But I knew I was moving toward my dream, toward the purpose God had given me. So I stayed focused on that purpose, which enabled me to take steps that I wouldn't normally have taken. With every step I took, it seemed like my faith grew, my boldness grew, and my knowledge of what to do grew to the place where I can literally now say I'm living my dream.

It's so important to take steps toward your dream. With every step forward, you will find the fear is unfounded. Every step forward, the fear lessens. As James 2:26 (Common English Bible) says, *"As the life-less body is dead, so faith without actions is dead."* So, begin preparing to take steps in faith toward your purpose. When you do that, you will find that God will never disappoint you.

Getting Started as an Entrepreneur

"How do I get started as an entrepreneur?" This is one of the most commonly asked questions that I hear in my line of work. To answer the question, let me tell you about my first two businesses.

The first business I ever formed was a simple carpet cleaning com-pany. This was back before you could easily pick up a carpet cleaner from Home Depot. The machines used to be quite scarce. I found a small, professional machine and bought it for $25 to start a carpet cleaning business.

However, that business turned out to be a massive failure. I lost money the entire time I ran the business. The good news is that I did sell the machine, so in that sense, I got my money back.

Years later, I decided to start another business. At that point in our lives, my wife, Becky, and I were already established with a reason-able income stream, but we went out on a limb and started a home magazine. (This was in the days before the Internet, back when home magazines were the rage.)

The magazine was called *Home Sweet Homes* and featured beau-tiful homes and their interiors. We had to buy one of those old film cameras with a special wide-angle lens so Becky could visit the homes and take pictures. That business was hugely successful for us. We ended up selling it and making good money during our ownership and at the sale.

So, what's my point? The point is that when it comes to stepping out and starting as an entrepreneur, you must be willing to fail. Actually, this same principle applies to anyone who wants to start or lead anything. You must be willing to take a risk! If you're not willing to take a risk for something you're doing in your life, then it's probably not something worth doing.

Jack Canfield, author, motivational speaker, corporate trainer, and entrepreneur, said, "Everything you want is on the other side of fear." Actor Will Smith put it this way, "God placed the best things in life on the other side of terror." The point is, if you can get to the other side of your fear—past all those things that are holding you back—then you will find the opportunity to do what I call *falling forward*. You'll experience noble failure and pick yourself up, and then you will learn to succeed. In that process, you will find the best things in your life.

I've had people of all ages ask how to get started in business, but they've played it safe their whole lives. As you get older, it gets hard to learn to take risks. Now when I say risks, I'm not talking about being stupid—especially if you're closer to my age. Always act in wisdom.

If you're young, I especially want you to read this carefully. When I was 28, a Christian psychologist gave me a life-changing piece of advice. I told this man that I wanted to do x, y, and z. He was a prominent figure on Christian television back then, so he caught me off guard with his response. He said, "Billy what's the worst thing that can happen?"

"Well, that's easy. The worst thing that can happen is that I can fail."

"Exactly!" he said. "That's the worst thing that can happen. You're only 28 years old, and you have a lot of years ahead of you if you need to pick yourself up and start over again."

Around that same time, my mentor told me that he had filed bankruptcy three times in his life before he became a success. And he was a wealthy man! The point is, to start a business and succeed, you must be willing to take risks. You have to follow your dreams and your God-given purpose—so don't be afraid to fail!

CHAPTER 1

THE LEADER
AND PURPOSE

You might be in transition right now, looking for what's next in your life. You might also just want to enhance where you are in life currently. Regardless of your present position, you should desire to engage in the will of God for your life because it's the race of your life.

In fact, we should want not only to engage in the will of God but to fulfill it. Many people have a vision of where they want to go or where they believe God is leading them. Yet in reality, those plans and visions don't always happen in the time or the way we thought they would happen. Therefore, we can get discouraged along the way.

In Hebrews 12:1-2, the Bible says:

Therefore we also, since we are surrounded by so great a cloud of witnesses, let us lay aside every weight and the sin which so easily ensnares us, and let us run with endurance the race that is set before us, looking unto Jesus the author and the finisher of our faith, who for the joy that was set before Him endured the cross, despising the shame, and is set down at the right hand of the throne of God.

It is possible to get weary and discouraged in your soul, but let's focus for a second on the phrase *"on the race that is set before us."* The Amplified Bible Classic Edition says, *"...let us run with patient endurance and steady and active persistence the appointed course of the race that is set before us."* The Living Bible translation says, *"and let us run with patience the particular race that God has set before us."*

Evidently, there is a race that God has for everyone, but it's unique to each one of us as individuals. That race, of course, is in parallel with the will of God for your life. This specific race that God has designed for you enables you to run to find, fulfill, and follow the will of God for your future. There is a particular course to which God has called you. Each person has individual finger prints and is unique before God. When it comes to running the race of your life successfully, I've found there are four steps you will need to process.

Step 1: Get in the Race. The first race you have to get into is the race at hand. Learn all you can learn, become all you can become, and then pick up some of the stuff around you. Not everything you need to succeed is a subject that will be taught. What I mean by that is that there will be some experiences or moments in your life that will teach you more than what you will learn in a classroom or seminar. Pay attention to those seasons.

The Bible says in 1 Corinthians 9:24 (AMPC), *"Do you not know that in a race all the runners compete, but [only] one receives the prize? So run [your race] that you may lay hold [of the prize] and make it yours."*

You need to be present in the race that is at hand and refuse to run half-heartedly. You want to run your race to win the prize! The apostle Paul writes in verse 26, *"Therefore I do not run uncertainly (without definite aim). I do not box like one beating the air and striking without an adversary."* In other words, you need to have a goal and focus in order to get there. Run with certainty!

Some people in life have completely checked out on the race that God has set before them. Usually this is because they have been hurt or mistreated. In any major city in the United States, there are plenty of homeless men and women under bridges and sometimes in churches. We pray for them, and we should help them. But many of those folk have checked out on the race they are destined to run because of the circumstances surrounding them. I'm not criticizing them. In reality, because of the hurt, the lies of the devil, or situations like addictions, they've checked out on the race of life.

You need to make sure you are focused on running the race God has for you. You cannot check out!

Step 2: Persist in the Face of Resistance. In the race of life, you don't have to be perfect. God has already finished the work in Christ. You will face resistance in this life, but you can overcome it with the grace of God.

I heard this quote for the first time in 1981, and it still impacts me today: "All good things are upstream." What does that mean? It means that when it comes to the good things in your life, you will encounter some resistance. Andrew Wommack, well-known minister, author, and Charis Bible College founder, says, "If you and the devil are going in the same direction, you're probably not going to run into a lot of resistance."

Think of a seed planted in soil. When that seed is in the soil, what does the soil provide for that seed? The first thing it provides is warmth and protection. The soil also provides basic nourishment: the minerals and moisture for the seed to be able to grow. And the soil provides resistance to make the seed strong. The weight of the soil on the seed provides resistance to the budding plant so when the plant breaks out of the kernel of the seed, it begins to move the weight of the soil.

One of the reasons God designed it that way is so when the plant ultimately breaks through the soil and comes out into the sunlight, it is strong enough to survive. In other words, when the wind blows hard and the sun beats down or the heavy rain pours, the plant can handle the elements that deliver what the seeds needs—moisture, warmth, and light. If the plant does not encounter resistance, the very elements intended to bring growth will actually bring death.

When you face resistance, know that God is preparing you. Most people give up at the first sign of difficulty; but if you persist, you will be able to move into the fullness of what God has planned for your life.

Step 3: Order over Perfection. God is not looking for you to be perfect. We know in Christ we have been made perfect in the righteousness of God. We know that in Christ we are new creatures. But most people think perfection means they can never make any mistakes in life; that is not the case. I believe God is looking for growth and improvement on its way to perfection or maturity.

The truth is, in this life you're going to make some mistakes. God knows it. You know it, and I know it. Sometimes things just happen, and it may not even be intentional. For example, when driving, have you ever pulled out in front of another car and you didn't mean to? Maybe you really didn't even see the car? I've done that before. The point is that we are not perfect. It's okay to make mistakes; it's expected. The most important thing is that there is order in your life.

There are five primary areas of your life that require order so you can prosper: family, feelings, faith, friends, and finances. *Order* means that you're not overly distracted in any one of these five areas. The Merriam-Webster Dictionary defines the word *distraction* as "an object that directs one's attention away from something else." There are many reasons why it's important not to be distracted. But the foremost reason is that the Holy Spirit might need to show you something—and if you're distracted, you won't see it.

Step 4: Promote Growth. John Maxwell said, "Most people live and die in a non-growth environment." Think about it. We go to school for twelve years, then we graduate high school. Some may move on to college for four years, and others still may go into a master's program. Even fewer people will graduate with doctorate degrees. The point is that most people stop learning the day they graduate from high school. After high school, most people step into some kind of job that may turn into a career. When you ask how long they've been at a company, they probably say, "I have 25 years of experience." That's not necessarily true. They may have one year of experience 25 times.

My wife's uncle was a great man. He was one of the gentlest human beings I've ever known. I asked him one time, "Uncle Donald, tell me what you do at Dow Chemical?" He said, "Well, I drive a forklift." I asked if he did anything else, and he told me sometimes they played cards. I then asked him if he was happy with his job, and he said he loved it. He went on to say that he retired after forty years of driving the forklift for Dow Chemical.

I love Uncle Donald, and I'm not criticizing him. However, he didn't have forty years of experience. He learned how to drive the forklift the first year. He loved it, and that's what he chose for his life's work. Don't deceive yourself. Most people live and die in a non-growth environment because they don't continue to advance.

The Race of Your Season

In order to find, follow, and fulfill the will of God, you need to get in the race of life. Then, you need to steward the season that you find yourself in to ultimately propel forward.

Hebrews 6:12 says that through faith and patience they inherited the promises. Keep your faith on where you're headed and what you're expecting. Apply patience to your faith so you stay in the season you're in. You don't abandon the baby before it's born. You stay with the incubation period until what God has for your life is birthed, and then you enter into a new season and a new time.

Pregnant with Purpose

Every season that you go through in life will be pregnant with purpose. Steward the season you're in to go into the next season.

I reached a level of financial independence in my life, but I did it for all the wrong reasons. I didn't realize God was letting me do that in order to teach me and show me a future I never even knew was possible. When I was building my wealth, God was preparing me for my purpose.

If we were to take all the money in the world and divide it up evenly, it would all be back in the same hands in a short period of time. Work on maturing in the season you're in so that you grow. After you mature and prepare in that season, God will start dropping things off at the job site of your life.

How do I know what God is doing? I look to see what kind of materials God is dropping off at my job site. When I was younger, I always used to try to kick down every metaphorical door of opportunity. Now, I wait for a door to open or a door to close, and then I steward it. When a door opens, even if I'm not comfortable with it, it's my job to walk through it.

But listen! I don't only watch the materials that God is dropping off at my job site; I also watch the people. I wouldn't be writing this book if it weren't for my initial relationship with certain people. I recognize the materials, and then God brings divine connections. Just about everything God does in your life, He does through relationships.

I was lying in bed one night when my phone rang. My wife asked who it was, but I didn't recognize the number. The area code was from Woodland Park, Colorado, which is where my good friend Andrew Wommack lived. I had a feeling it might be Andrew, and my wife told me I better call him back. Yet, it was 9:30 at night so I wasn't really sure I wanted to do that. My wife said, "You're going to get up, put your regular clothes on, sit on the couch, and talk to him." I saluted her, got up, and called Andrew.

He apologized for calling so late, but he told me that he had been up praying. He asked if I would want to be on his board of directors, which is not what I was expecting at all. I got up off the couch and approached my wife who was still in bed. I told her that I was going to turn him down, but she reminded me what I am telling you here—wait to see what God is dropping off at your job site. Steward the materials, steward the relationships, and mature in each season.

Spiritual protocol and honor will hold you in place like an anchor on a ship in a storm. They will hold you in place until you can see the wind laid down and the sun begin to shine. This passage in Luke truly helped me understand being anchored in a season of maturing:

> *Whoever can be trusted with very little can also be trusted with much, and whoever is dishonest with very little will also be dishonest with much. So if you have not been trustworthy in handling worldly wealth, who will trust you with true riches? And if you have not been trustworthy with someone else's property, who will give you property of your own?* (Luke 16:10-12 NIV)

Meditate on that Scripture regardless of your current season. The first thing Jesus says in that Scripture passage is, "*Whoever can be trusted with very little can also be trusted with much.*" That means you have to be faithful in small things that nobody else can see you doing—the stuff nobody thinks is important. That can include cleaning the bathrooms and vacuuming the carpet. Begin by being faithful in what is least or seems little.

The Race of Your Destiny

Proverbs 19 and 20 speak about the purpose of God. Proverbs 20:5 (NIV) says, *"The purposes of a person's heart are deep waters, but one who has insight draws them out."* Let's consider a life application of this Scripture.

I came from South Texas where we caught a two types of fish—largemouth bass and crappie. When we fished for largemouth bass, we used worms or other lures as bait. When we fished for crappie, we used little jigs.

Later I lived on the coast, so we would catch red fish, speckled trout, and flounder, which meant we used different bait for each yet again. Eventually, I moved to Colorado where it took me a long time to really learn how to fly-fish.

In all these places, you can catch some fish in the warmer weather on the top. However, the truth is that 90 percent of all fish are caught deeper in the water, and 98 percent of all big fish are caught even deeper still.

It's the same with purpose. The purposes in a person's heart are like deep water, but a person of insight or understanding will draw them out. Most of us think that God is going to show up and just slap us upside the head to give us purpose and vision. Most of us are looking for a Damascus Road experience as Paul had (see Acts 9:1-31). Yet, God's Word is telling us that purposes run deep, and we must draw them out.

Think about this. You're in at least three races: the race of life; the race of your current season; and the race of your destiny or your purpose.

I remember the first time God led me outside of ministry and over into business in a big way. Honestly, I misread the whole situation. I thought it was all about me and what I could get. Then I found out it had nothing to do with me, what I had done, or what I had made. That was just a bunch of self-centered junk.

God had a purpose in teaching me and one of the first things I learned was how to handle big money. Once that first big "fish" came up, God showed me how important it was for me to learn about money because of a new destiny into which He was taking me. When that happened, I learned to think differently, talk differently, and see differently.

I also had to learn to stop trying to go back to where I was before. It's human nature to want to return to what's familiar and comfortable, but that's not where your purpose lies. If I had gone back, which I was sorely tempted to do, I wouldn't be doing what I'm doing today. You wouldn't be reading this book right now.

Four Steps to Knowing What's Next in Life

I have learned that God takes us through four steps when we are looking for what's next in our lives. The following are some ways you can draw out purpose and prepare for what's ahead.

1. Preparation

Anytime you step into what's next in your life, there always will have been a season of preparation. I remember reading the story of Jehoiachin, who was freed from prison. As I read the passage, I remember saying under my breath, "Lord, why did this happen? All the other kings were there, but You only elevated and favored Jehoiachin. You make it clear throughout Scriptures that You don't show favoritism. So why would You show favor to Jehoiachin and not the other kings? Why was he unique?"

After praying, I went back to study the meaning of Jehoiachin's name using a reference book called Hitchcock Bible Names. Jehoiachin's name means "preparation." It was a very common practice in ancient times to name people prophetically or to rename them in stories based on how they lived. Jehoiachin's name tells us something important. He was in prison for thirty-seven years before he was lifted up and shown favor. Yet, since his name meant "preparation," I think it's safe to assume he prepared during those thirty-seven years. I believe he kept his heart in the right place and his mind active. And I believe that Jehoiachin never gave up but continually prepared himself for the next step.

2. Shift in Peace and Presence

I remember when the Lord was leading me into real estate full time. I already owned quite a few investment properties, but it seemed the Lord was shifting my direction. I felt the peace of God start shifting me and work I liked before I didn't like anymore. At first, I got this uneasy feeling on the inside and thought it was just my flesh. But I just kept feeling the shift.

Even areas where I had really felt the presence of God in that season, I no longer felt the same presence. Those areas no longer meant the same thing to me. In fact, for two years I did not want to stand up and teach anybody. Whether it was business or preaching, I did not want to do it. I felt a distaste for certain things, and I had to go through a process of mind renewal.

3. Confirmation from Other People

When you're moving into a new season, there will be provision. Where God guides, He provides. There also will be affirmation from others. Whenever God leads you into new seasons, He also will provide godly mentors and advisors to help you know how to take those next steps.

However, you have to be careful with whose opinions you allow to matter to you. Consider the opinions from the five or so people closest people to you. When they start seeing you shift, they will confirm what God is pulling toward you. Sometimes God speaks to other people, so make sure you're listening with discernment.

4. God Leads in Small Steps

Typically when God leads you, it will be in small steps. The will of God is usually not eighteen steps from where you are now. Start by putting your toes in the water, and then submerge your feet. Before you know it, you are waist deep in what God has for you. As you focus on taking the next right step, before you realize it, you will have walked up a full staircase.

Get the Timing Right

Most people misunderstand timing because they think that God is arbitrarily giving and taking. God has already done everything He's going to do on the cross. That's why Roman's 12:2 says, *"Do not be conformed to this world, but be transformed by the renewing of your mind, that you may prove what is that good and acceptable and perfect will of God."*

King David said, *"The boundary lines have fallen for me in pleasant places"* (Psalm 16:6 NIV). God has no favorites, so if He'll give David the proper boundaries for his life, then God has a boundary for your life too.

Paul says it this way, *"We, however, will not boast beyond measure, but within the limits of the sphere which God appointed us"* (2 Corinthians 10:13). There is a measure God has put around each one of our lives that we are supposed to fulfill. It took me years to learn that. I thought I was supposed to have what everybody else had. What is God saying your boundary is? What is God saying your measure is?

Remember that we're reading Hebrews chapter 12, which says, *"... the race that is set before us."* That race set before you is your destiny and purpose, and your race has a boundary or a measure.

When I use the term *boundary*, I don't mean that you are limited. I don't know what your boundary is, but I know that your boundaries have fallen to you in pleasant places. People often try early on to jump right into their full boundary or destiny, which is like giving a 10-year-old the keys to the family car. They couldn't handle it if they got there, which is why you need to grow and mature in each season.

Learn to discern the times and the season. That will allow you to function in patience, and through faith in patience, you inherit the promises. If you understand where you're supposed to be but there are some parts you don't like, don't worry about it. Your boundaries have fallen to you in pleasant places.

I declare over you like the apostle Paul said that you won't press beyond your measure. If you press beyond your measure that's self-promotion and disobedience. If you press beyond your measure, then you won't get what you're supposed to get in the maturation process. You won't get what you need that qualifies and prepares you for the next step.

Finding your purpose and fulfilling God's will for your life can feel daunting. But keep in mind the things I've taught you in this chapter. Get in the race of your life, steward the race of your season, and draw out the race of your destiny.

CHAPTER 2

THE LEADER AND COURAGE

Faith shows the reality of what we hope for;
it is the evidence of things we cannot see.
(Hebrews 11:1 New Living Translation)

There are three characteristics that define and build great leaders: confidence, courage, and tenacity. Let's look at each.

Confidence. This is a word that every leader needs to try on for size. A leader is someone who can inspire action in others, but in order to do that, you need to win people's trust. You need to have confidence in yourself and the dreams you're trying to get people to envision.

History is full of examples of leaders who had strong leadership skills but bad intentions. Think Adolf Hitler, Jim Jones, Charles Ponzi. These men were not short on charisma, and they won people's trust and loyalty without deserving it. So let me ask, if these infamous people with malicious dreams had confidence to do what they did, why shouldn't you have confidence to do what you know is right?

History is also full of examples of leaders who had strong leadership skills and used them to inspire people to do great things. Consider Winston Churchill, Helen Keller, and Smith Wigglesworth, for example. The world is also full of examples of leaders who lead strongly in whatever small role they were given. Those are the people down the street who work a normal 9-5 job and excel in raising their children. It's the pastor who may have a small church but leads a congregation whose lives are bettered daily by his work. It's the mom at home tending to her special needs child.

Whatever position you are in right now, it's time to build your confidence. This is fuel that allows you to start your engine running. Whether you're trying to start a new organization, rebirth yourself as a better leader for your pre-existing role, or just get better at leading your family, you need fuel to run on. Starting the engine is the first step that will build momentum.

Entrepreneurship operates out of the idea that you have something to offer the world. In other words, you have a business plan that differs from others' plans. You see a market that is missing something you could give. You have or know something people want. It takes confidence to move from thinking such things to creating a business plan.

This same concept applies to any area of leadership. As a parent, you believe you have something to offer your children: training, love, safety. As a pastor, you have something you're offering to your congregation: care, guidance, counseling. Whatever the situation, it starts with you. What do you have to offer? I promise you, God has given you a purpose and a plan. He has given you innate gifts that you can offer the world.

Steve Wozniak is the cofounder of Apple with Steve Jobs. Wozniak designed and built Apple 1, the first personal computer. This is a man who ventured bravely into an unexplored territory.

Wozniak said, "If you love what you do and are willing to do what it takes, it's within your reach. And it'll be worth every minute you spend alone at night, thinking and thinking about what it is you want to design or build. It'll be worth it, I promise."[1]

To Wozniak, it's all about passion and confidence. He believed in his abilities and went for it. He had confidence. But there's an important distinction to make—it's the difference between success and failure. Wozniak had confidence and, loads of it, but he wasn't caught up with *hubris*.

Hubris is defined as exaggerated pride or self-confidence—a great or foolish amount of pride or confidence. In other words, Wozniak wasn't falling into the trap of hubris—unable to partner with anyone or receive criticism. Steve Jobs was right by his side going to the next step—selling the computer. Together, they started one of the most important companies of our time.

There are three downfalls of hubris:

1. Hubris believes that you don't need anyone else. It is confidence so exaggerated and inflated that it causes people to think they can do anything and everything all alone. They think, *Why have someone else join me when I can do it better?* This is a trap that leads to failure.

2. Hubris also prevents people from foreseeing hiccups. They are so hyper-confident in the plans that they make, that they assume nothing can go wrong. Instead of looking at all angles of an issue, ironing out the plan for the best option, hubris causes leaders to charge forward with the first thing that comes to mind. Hubris causes leaders to neglect setting up checks and balances in the system; then when a problem arises, there is no system to fix it.

3. Last, hubris prevents a leader from accepting failure with grace. Failure will happen at some point to some degree. It's simply part of life and learning and growing. When failure happens, the over-pressurized bubble of hubris can pop. You find yourself in a pit of depression, unable to get back up and try again. Or sometimes hubris is so blind to failure that it will keep brazenly pushing forward, not learning from mistakes and causing more damage.

In place of hubris, try on these three adjectives that describe the word *confident:* 1) sure of oneself; 2) having no uncertainty about one's own abilities; 3) bold.[2]

Again, this is a delicate walk. Confidence is the energy we feel when we wake up and tackle something difficult. It is a healthy belief in self and ideas that allows us to explore a new territory. Confidence says, "I can do this. I will need help. I will to need to learn along the way. And there are probably moments of failure ahead. But I can do this."

Being *courageous* is possessing the quality of mind or spirit that enables a person to face difficulty, danger, pain, and more without fear. It's bravery.[3]

It takes courage to talk to investors about your business plan or to switch on the "OPEN" sign after an opening day flop. A strong leader controls fear and steps forward to face the difficult climb. It's showing up to counseling with your spouse. It's grounding your child for the first time. It's stepping back onto that pulpit after a church goer has critiqued you harshly. It's looking fear in the face and stepping forward anyway.

Tenacious means being unwilling to accept defeat or stop doing something. The truth is, failure and rejection are part of the climb. The question is, what will you do after? Get back up or stay down? If you're feeling bruised from a failed venture, I understand. I have experienced failure more times than I can count. But I got back up and kept going until I met success.

These three words we've looked at are actually steps you will take on your journey. You need *confidence* to get started, *courage* to push through when it gets scary, and *tenacity* to get back up when you fall.

Let's not forget about the example of the greatest leader of all—Jesus. He was one person who inspired generations after generations with the truth of His words. He never doubted His God-ordained purpose, and neither should you. Yes, your path might change and develop as you learn. Your purpose might grow and shift. Humans are not God, after all! But you should never doubt that God has a purpose for you. Have faith in God's promises. He has chosen you and appointed you that you should go and bear fruit. Be confident in your faith that He has given you a gift to share with the world.

John 15:16 says:

> *You did not choose Me, but I chose you and appointed you so that you might go and bear fruit—fruit that will last—and so that whatever you ask in My name the Father will give you.*

Digging Trenches

The New American Standard Bible version of 2 Kings 3:16-17 states:

> *He said, "Thus says the Lord, 'Make this valley full of trenches.' For thus says the Lord, 'You shall not see wind nor shall you see rain; yet that valley shall be filled with water….'"*

In these two verses, God has the people doing the hard labor of preparation—digging trenches. When the way is prepared, God delivers. When I started WealthBuilders in 2014, there were a lot of hard days for my team and me. We did not often reap profits from our efforts. But what we were doing was building trenches. We were laying the foundations of a new business, strong foundations, so that sustainability would follow. The hard work and long hours are the digging and the products and programs and systems we assembled—the trenches. Then we waited for water. Let me tell you, sure enough, God's blessings came and our trenches filled.

Waiting is an important component of this digging trenches process. Especially in this day and age, the virtue of patience has faded. Having spent time in developing nations, I've seen firsthand the time it takes people to do the basic tasks of living. While we turn on an oven or start the washer, they start a fire with charcoal and scrub their clothes with lye. What I might spend ten minutes doing, they spend an hour doing. The advances we've made are amazing and suddenly we have time to dedicate to intellectual pursuits. But this freedom has also come with a negative societal consequence—we don't wait. If a web page doesn't download in a nanosecond, we're infuriated and close everything. There is a sense of entitlement that is going to ruin us. We expect things to be quickly handed to us and become frustrated when that's not how it works.

The reality is that while many things in our lives run at high-speed, developing character and intellect does not. These require patience.

Patience as you wait should not look like passivity, however. A major component of digging trenches in your own life is to invest in yourself, and you should be investing in yourself. Digging trenches by investing in yourself looks like getting an education, discovering what you're passionate about and talented at, and or taking an unpaid internship to gain experience. It's having daily meditations on God's Word and in prayer so that you are aligned in His will. These things take time, and frankly, they take work. It can feel aimless at times. But that's all part of digging the trench. By putting the hours and work in here and now, you can be assured that success and blessing will come later.

This investing is also true in other life areas such as investing in a relationship or a community project. In the beginning of investing in these areas, it can feel like trudging along. It's hard to earn trust and develop a relationship. But once the path is laid, it becomes easy to move forward. Momentum starts to build.

Above everything else about digging trenches is the fact that we must have *hope*. Hope is an indispensable character trait for the hard work of digging trenches. Yet, the point is that we dig trenches *because* we have hope for a better future. It is not a naive hope that trusts in nothing, rather it is a hope that trusts in our efforts and our God.

In other words, you get an education because you have hope that it will lead to a good job. You ask someone out because you have hope that the date will lead to a relationship. You volunteer because you have hope that your effort will help change your community. Without hope, forward motion is pointless. There is no growth. But with hope—by digging trenches—we believe in a better tomorrow.

Invest in Yourself

Watching the deep patience of those in developing nations is not the only lesson I've learned overseas. There is a universal experience that every person with a Western upbringing experiences when he or she enters a developing nation—the flurry of requests for money. It's awkward and overwhelming at times. You want to help, but realistically doling out cash does little in the big picture. You can't help everyone in this way. This reality is one of the reasons we started Tricord Global—we wondered how we could help people on a global scale.

I felt this pressure to help the first several times I experienced solicitation. Wherever I turned, people noticed I was an American and immediately imagined their culture's stock photo of what an American is. As a result, they would boldly run up and say, "Hey, give me fifty kwacha!" (Kwacha is the currency in Malawi, a previous Tri-cord Global location.)

A Malawian cultural trainer explained that I had experienced only half of this encounter and walked me through the other half. To us, requests for money feel personal. We feel guilty that we can't help. Yet the trainer pointed out that these people weren't putting their hopes and dreams in me—a weight that you or I might naturally assume. Instead, they are constantly on the lookout for ways to raise their status in the world—ways to feed the family, start a business, buy a goat. They see us as *opportunities*. In their mindset, *Why not go for it?* As they see it, the worst case is that they get rejected. On the other hand, just maybe they get cash for some cooking oil and plastic wrap to start a self-sustaining business.

When I realized this, I was amazed. This shameless, take-chances mindset is remarkable to someone like me raised in a culture of protocol. Here I was, learning something valuable and insightful from a people group the world largely dismisses—the impoverished.

Here's my takeaway lesson from that experience—be bold. As a leader, you need to infuse confidence into everything you do. People in developing nations have an innate sense of their self-worth. Frankly, they need it on a deeper level than we do—they're fighting for food, education, and life. This attitude inspires their boldness to ask.

Similarly, you can learn to overcome cultural restraint. I don't mean that you should go around breaking every societal rule, but I do mean that you should learn to push back. Learn how to ask and ask well, because it doesn't hurt to try. You may find the help you're looking for, or you might gain a reference, and thereby grow your network. Remember, the worst thing that can happen is that you get turned away. And that's not the end of the world at all.

I have also learned to jump at every opportunity. No matter who you are or where you live, I bet you have a dream. Yet sometimes we don't jump at the opportunities life brings. If you have dreams of opening a restaurant and happen to meet a possible investor, jump! There will always be a voice of fear in your head that says, *Maybe the time isn't right.* That voice will never change if you don't change it.

Sometimes we need courage in the face of real dangers. But most of the time, the dangers aren't real. They're simply a manifestation of a fearful imagination. Whether you're putting off school or biding your time at your current position, it's time to really analyze the timing and jump. Next year you will only be older. Remember that failure is just a bump in the road, not the end of the path.

I was also in awe of how these people in developing nations bounced back. When I said, "Sorry, I can't help," do you think those individuals went away and sulked? No. They kept their eyes open for the next opportunity. Rejection is the same no matter what world you live in. I've experienced it time and time again, and so will you.

The man asking you for cash at the local market hasn't put all his eggs in your basket. He has a plan and options. He's looking for work or already working. When he walks away, he's moved on to the next plan. Adopt this attitude, and you will find peace in your life. It's easy to keep your eggs in one basket. It's easy to throw yourself a pity party. Instead, keep your options open and keep moving.

Foster Creativity

The best way to keep your options open is to foster your creativity. Leadership can be exhausting. You will confront strong temptations to constantly check your phone, lock yourself in the office, and do everything by yourself. But to be healthy and successful, you should actually pace yourself and take a step back. Foster creativity with some of these following tips, and your daily routine will become enjoyable instead of drudgery.

1. *Dedicate an hour a day to being technology free.* There are a couple of ways to do this. If you're a morning person, don't even look at your phone when you first wake up. If an emergency happened, there's nothing you can really do until you're up and going anyway. If you're more of an evening person, then take the hour before bed. Or maybe dedicate a meal to being technology free!

No matter when you schedule this time, it is going to stimulate your creativity and energize you. That moment when you gear up to shut off the phone and put it away can be hard, but it will be worth it to allow yourself some mental space.

2. *Be out and about.* From taking walks to reading in coffee shops, being out and about is a wonderful way to stay mentally stimulated. Solitude and nature also can be wonderful, creative stimulants. In fact, Charles Dickens went on a 20-mile walk every day! The fresh air wakes your mind, and the solitude allows your thoughts to flourish.

Similarly, going to museums or coffee shops or bookstores can stimulate creativity. Being around people and out and about in different scenarios can reconnect you to what people want. It might get you thinking about services you could offer that would make things easier for your clientele. Or maybe it stimulates a new idea for an outreach at your church. Either way, these two practices can help reset your brain daily. It is important to make a designated time for your mind to flush out ideas and gain new inspiration.

3. *Network with fellow* _____. Fill in the blank. Whatever title you associate with yourself or hope to have tacked on some day, hang out with those people. Polish your social media presence and get to know others in your field. By connecting on LinkedIn or Facebook, for example, you can start a conversation and learn from each other.

Get to know people in your area who are doing what you want to do and see if you can partner in any way. If a partnership doesn't work out, at least you can bounce ideas off a new friend you have made in the game. Stay active in your community and online. These people you network with will inspire you and be a resource to you.

4. *Prioritize what energizes you.* When my WealthBuilders team told me how energized I seemed after personal coaching sessions, they encouraged me to prioritize that as part of my schedule. I was surprised they noticed this, but they were completely right. Making sure I have a frequent dose of coaching keeps me energized and ready for the things that don't energize me.

So, figure out what area of your life and career really wakes you up and fills you with joy and energy. Then prioritize this and make it part of your weekly schedule. This dose of energy will keep you going through the difficult times.

Direct Your Future

When I retired, I had no idea that my life and goals would change so much. I had made it! *Retirement.* That freedom we long for as a culture was mine; and yet, I was bored and unhappy. In fact, my wife, Becky, finally told me to get out and go to work! So I started thinking about where I wanted to be in five years. Here I am, well over five years later and leading multiple businesses, teaching, coaching, and most importantly, enjoying my life. To keep yourself on a healthy track, try using these following three tools to evaluate where you are and where you are going:

1. *Bucket List.* At the end of your life, you don't want to be full of regrets. So be proactive today by coming up with a list of things you truly want to do. This can be anything including: fill a journal, climb Mount Everest, cultivate a garden, visit Ireland. No matter how big or small, write it down. (In fact, I personally like to include a few small things to check off easily.) Keep this list somewhere you will see it regularly—driver's seat visor, nightstand, bathroom mirror. Keeping the list accessible will continually motivate you to incorporate those goals into your life.

2. *Personal Growth Goal.* In a way, we attempt to set goals every year on January 1st. But it has become a national joke that no one ever follows through. So instead, find a time frame that works for you. One goal for a year is easy to put off, because a year is so long. Instead, try developing a goal for a month or three months. I even suggest starting with something small and achievable just to get you in a personal growth mindset.

Write a specific goal down and place it in your shower, on your work computer, in your phone background—anywhere you'll see at least once a day. Practice this growth step daily for your time limit. And then, when you feel it become habitual, choose another step to work on for three months or whatever the designated timeframe. One month you might practice drinking enough water and the next you start cleaning up your self-doubting language. Keep practicing, and it will become a habit. Not only that, but the attitude of continually developing will inspire you to tackle bigger and bigger things.

3. *The X-Year Plan.* The infamous five-year plan is surprisingly relevant. High school and college graduates feel overwhelmed with this idea because there is still so much that can change depending on their first career. But especially when you are settling into your first job, or have been settled for decades, this is a great thing to think about.

Your plan might look like getting your company to a point of self-sustainability in five years. For another, it might look like starting a family in the next three years. It could be getting a position as a lead pastor in one year. Look at your life in an annual scale and figure out where you're going. Once you know that, you can start from there.

Defining Wealth

A friend of the family once visited one of Tricord's Malawian contacts. As she visited our contact's house and sat down to eat, she took in what it means to be wealthy in Lilongwe, Malawi. As a respected, wealthy citizen, the family had a nice house with a kitchen and bathroom. Yet she noticed that instead of toilet paper, an old notebook was strung up in the bathroom with pages torn.

It is interesting to think that the idea of wealth can be so universal and yet look so different. The majority of people in the United States wouldn't even think about using a notebook in the bathroom. Toilet paper is basically a given in the Western world. But in Malawi, that doesn't fit into their view of wealth.

So what is wealth? Wealth is relative, specific, and symbolic. As you develop yourself into a strong leader, you will need to define wealth for yourself.

To me, wealth is good health, a connected family, and success in my ventures. To younger people I know, wealth is freedom from school debt, a new car, and a happy marriage. To our Malawian contact, it is a solid home, a television, and a wife and kids. There is no one true definition of a wealthy person.

Wealth always reflects back onto us. It is a symbol of achievement, success, respect, care, and love. When I see the good things in my life, I appreciate them because of what they say to me, "Well done, you made it." Our contact in Malawi sees his home as a symbol of his status and respect in his community. Similarly, your car or phone symbolize something deeper when you consider them as part of what makes you wealthy.

Think about it. What does wealth symbolize to you? What does wealth specifically look like for you? When you think of your life plan, what does wealth mean when looking at the big picture?

End the Love-Hate Relationship with Money

> "A wise man should have money in his head, but not in his heart." —Jonathan Swift

As leaders, money is a topic we have to focus on. In many ways, it seems like our culture drives on money; and yet, it might be one of the least reflected upon aspects of modern life. Loved? Yes. Hated? Yes. Obsessed over? Certainly. Hoarded? All too often. But how often do we reflect on what money is *supposed* to mean?

No matter your vision or dream, money is likely going to be a factor. Whether it's tithes, the family budget, or getting capital for a business, chances are you will need to deal with money often. Therefore, it's important that we put the concept of money in its place. Whether you love or hate money, either extreme is giving it too much credit and influence on your life. When seen in the clear light of day, money is neither as beautiful nor as horrible as we make it out to be. (For a full breakdown of this concept, check out my book, *Money Mastery*.)

I want to propose an active view of money. Think of money as potential energy, as opportunity. See it for what it is—a resource. Money is never something that can bring satisfaction in and of itself.

The following are tips for making money work for you:

Never disconnect your dollar from what you want to do with it. Money is simply a tool you can use to do things. One of the best ways to keep money from taking control of your life is to give it a job to do. Money that sits around purposelessly is wasted potential. I'm not saying you should spend every dollar that comes your way! Saving money is wise. Building a safety net of funds is wise. But every dollar we set aside should have a purpose. If we're building a stockpile out of fear, or just out of habit, then money has mastery over us. It's time to reconnect those dollars to a purpose.

Make sure your value system and your budget match up. Another way to make money work for you is to let it reflect your priorities. Take a look at what you spend, both personally and in your business or vision. Does your spending reflect your values and goals, or does it tell a different story? You can give plenty of justifications for your decisions, but the numbers won't lie to you. Going forward, make your bank statement reflect your heart, not just your circumstances and fears.

Pass it on. Money doesn't determine who you are. It's not part of your identity. Why should having more make you act like a different person? Live your life sincerely and learn to use money in a way that sustains that.

I believe this wisdom is worth passing on, because as a nation our obsession with money is hurting our ability to live meaningful and productive lives. Investors and entrepreneurs should be at the forefront of thoughts on money. We should have the loudest voice about its role. Let's think sustainability. In line with the old proverb, teaching someone to view and use money wisely is teaching the person to fish, not giving a fish for a day. With our money and the lessons we learn about how to use it properly, we can change the world. That's true leadership!

Staying Grounded

In the process of digging trenches, there will be some hard days. There will be times when it feels like it's too much work. That's why it's important to not overdo it. We all need to make sure we give ourselves a chance to kick back, get with our loved ones, and do something that gives us life and energy.

Physical rest and time with family are essential. But the reality is that it can be pretty easy for us to put in more hours than what is required and to shoulder more responsibility than is necessary. On top of that, running a small business or a household can be like piloting a small boat on an ocean—you will feel all the hard bumps. For example, my plans in our office can be offset by factors as far ranging as the weather in Africa to local politics.

Even on a balanced schedule we need constant spiritual and mental refreshments, and we need them as we work. If we can only find peace in escaping our responsibilities, it's time to take a look and find out why that is. The following are three practices to keep you anchored when the storm is raging:

Remember whom you serve. Few things are more dangerous than losing vision—and nothing can make us lose vision quicker than worrying about our immediate achievement and prosperity. Ironically, nothing keeps us anchored like our destination. It is easier to stay afloat heading toward somewhere than treading water.

Ask yourself why you got into your field in the first place. Whose words inspired you to take the course you did or create what you created? What needs and what calling do you serve? Take some time to go back to that original muse that inspired your efforts, whether it was words, an event, an experience, or a relationship. You might find that muse to be just as inspiring now as you did the first time.

Know where you end and others begin. Overcommitting has a dual meaning: 1) Committing to more jobs than you can physically handle; and 2) Committing to jobs you aren't quite qualified to do. We often overcommit because it seems heartless to ignore someone's plea. Working like this keeps us feeling out of control of our lives, motivated by guilt, and manipulated instead of working toward our vision with compassion.

Chaplains in the military live by a code to keep from overcommitting in a job that entails enormous stress; they are to either provide the service or find someone who can appropriately meet the needs. When a chaplain encounters someone who has true psychological issues, he or she doesn't overextend by trying to help. Rather, the individual is sent to a psychologist—someone who is trained to handle deep psychological issues.

The best way to preserve a relationship is often to bring someone more qualified into the conversation. It shows respect for everyone involved, including yourself. Start building a portfolio of references and colleagues as a resource for your market. You won't have the capacity, either in time or in ability, to take on every project that comes your way. Try to focus on the ones that are most closely aligned with your vision and abilities. Then get a trusted reference to take on others.

Take stock of what is permanent. If the market dries up, your novel is rejected, relationships break up, or any other unpredictable factor brings everything to a halt, what do you have left? Probably a great deal.

I read a story that Robert Schuller shared over 35 years ago about a man who came to him and told him that he had lost everything. His business had gone bankrupt and his wife had left him. He came to Reverend Schuller in great distress and said it was all over; he had lost everything. Reverend Schuller asked him if he could still see. The man said yes, of course. Reverend Schuller asked several more similar questions such as could he still think? Was he healthy enough to work with his hands? Was his hearing good? The man had answered yes to all of the questions. Then Reverend Schuller said, "Well, you haven't lost everything yet. You still have great potential and much to live for!"

Going into doomsday mode every time trouble comes is an insult to those dedicated to your well-being. Consider your visions and beliefs, your family and relatives, a supportive community at your church or in the neighborhood, good friends you know will always have your back, or even just a chance to simplify life. If you truly can't think of anything positive in your life right now, perhaps there are more important works in your near future to invest your time in. It will be the most important investment you ever make.

Endnotes

1. Steve Wozniak, *iWoz: Computer Geek to Cult Icon: How I Invented the Personal Computer, Co-Founded Apple, and Had Fun Doing It* (New York: W.W. Norton & Company, 2006).

2. *Confidence*, defined by Dictionary.com.

3. *Courage*, defined by Dictionary.com.

4. *Tenacious*, defined by Cambridge Dictionaries Online.

CHAPTER 3

THE LEADER AND DISAPPOINTMENT

The Spirit of Disappointment

When I was in high school in the early 1970s, it was the "in" thing to sneak up on someone and punch them in the arm with your middle finger bent over into a pointed position. It would cause the muscle in the arm to form a bump and twitch uncontrollably. Kids would grab their arm to stop the twitching, but it didn't help. We called this "frogging" a person. The worst part, though, was how sore your arm would be the next day. In fact, in a particularly potent frogging incident, your arm could be sore for a week.

Life has a way of frogging us. It sneaks up on us and with its middle finger bent over and inflicts the "frogs" of disappointment. We don't see it coming, and yet in some cases, the pain of it sticks with us our entire lives. This is what a spirit of disappointment is—the long-term pain of unfulfilled expectations.

The dictionary says *to disappoint* means "to fail to satisfy the hopes or expectations of." Basically, it's unmet expectations. We become disappointed when we have expectations that go unsatisfied. Analyzing the etymology of the word *disappointment* shows us that it literally means "to separate from appointment."

If two people have an appointment to have coffee at ten o'clock and one person misses that appointment, the appointment didn't happen. One party didn't show up, and the plan to meet was unable to be carried out. Sometimes circumstances in our lives don't happen as we think they should, and our expectations go unmet. We feel let down. In other words, our dreams, expectations, goals, and hopes miss the appointment we thought we would have. This results in disappointment.

Many people carry disappointment with them for years—or even their entire lives. They don't make any new resolutions or set any new goals because they don't want to be disappointed again. Because of the frustration of disappointment, they don't move forward in their faith. They allow a spirit of disappointment to put a ceiling on their lives.

People carrying disappointment usually aren't aware that it's even there, let alone slowly chipping away at their belief system as time passes. Disappointments that are allowed to fester can cause us to possess disabling beliefs about God, ourselves, and others. These disabling beliefs not only dishonor God, but they also hurt us and those around us. When we carry those disappointments with us over time, we begin to identify with the hurts from our past rather than the promises of God for our future.

Once, while preparing for a new year, I asked myself, *Why weren't my expectations higher for the past year?* It took some time, but I finally realized that I was carrying disappointments from previously unmet expectations. It affected my ability to expect and believe better for the future.

As you develop yourself into a strong leader, it's important to tackle the issues of disappointment in your life. At that time in my life, I was letting disappointment affect how I planned out goals for my future. As a leader, you will set goals and lead others. If your own spirit of disappointment is pinning you down, how will you successfully lead others on their paths? How will you react when a person you are leading lets you down? You need to overcome the spirit of disappointment in your own life so that you can be prepared for the many challenges of leadership.

Disappointment Makes the Heart Sick

Proverbs 13:12 says, *"Hope deferred makes the heart sick, but when the desire comes, it is a tree of life."* The Living Bible translation says: *"Hope deferred makes the heart sick, but when dreams come true at last, there is life and joy."* Notice that it says *"when dreams come true...."* We agree, of course, that when our dreams come true, it is exciting because an expectation is met! But when it is put off, our hearts become sick.

Take a moment to really think about that. When your body is ill, everything around you looks gloomy. That's what happens to us when our hope is deferred. Our hearts get sick when we allow disappointment to stay with us. In other words, we fail to function at the level that we should because we are carrying the hurt of unfulfilled expectations.

Some people have become so accustomed to carrying disappointment with them that they think feeling that way is normal. A friend of mine who had been dealing with an illness for a while told me that he didn't know how poorly he felt until he felt well again. It's common for people carrying a spirit of disappointment to not realize how far off they are from "normal." They think that feeling spiritually and emotionally awful *is* normal.

What does Proverbs 13:12 mean when it says that hope deferred makes the heart sick? In this instance, to be *sick* means "to be rubbed or worn away." Whether it's your carpet or your socks, if something is rubbed enough, eventually the threads will be worn bare, and it will become weak. When our spirits have been rubbed and worn away, we don't set new goals, dream new dreams, or let God speak to our hearts. Instead, we allow those past disappointments to remain in us.

The Bible says this sickens our heart. It rubs and wears away at our belief system and our expectations so that we end up being spiritually and emotionally fragile. We carry disappointment and hurt with us everywhere we go. It keeps rubbing away until finally it doesn't matter how good any news is, it still feels bad. Finally, the threads break—your heart is sick.

God wants your heart to be strong, but it takes more than just positive thinking to keep your heart strengthened. You must daily feed on the promises of the Word of God. In fact, I encourage you to find specific promises of God about whatever has caused disappointment in your life and meditate on His promises. Joshua 1:8 says:

> *This Book of the Law shall not depart from your mouth, but you shall mediate in it day and night.... For then you will make your way prosperous, and then you will have good success.*

I believe in positive thinking, but God wants our spirit to be strong, not just our mind. Psalm 112:7 (NIV) says, *"They* [people's whose hearts are established] *will have no fear of bad news; their hearts are steadfast, trusting in the Lord."* The King James version says, *"He shall not be afraid of evil tidings: his heart is fixed* [established], *trusting in the Lord.*" The very opposite of this verse is to cringe when evil tidings come. We cringe because we are so fragile as a result of the disappointments we have carried with us. They are constantly wearing away at our hearts and our belief systems.

It is unhealthy to live your life with so much fear and disappointment from past occurrences that you cringe every time something negative happens. You cannot do what God has called you to do, with a sick heart carrying hurt and disappointment. God wants your heart to be strong and established so when He speaks, you can do what He's purposed for you to do. When God calls you to step up and lead your church, you are free to do it without fear. When you hire your first employee, you are able to do it free from baggage of past disappointments.

We have all been disappointed at one time or another. The older we become the more opportunities there are to experience disappointment. There's a reason people say, "Life happens." But in Matthew 7, Jesus told a parable that addresses life happening: the same torrential rains and floods, or disappointments, came upon two different houses. Even though each house was presented with the same challenges, the two houses held up differently because their foundations were different. Some people experience a flood in their life and it rolls off of them like water. Others, however, work hard not to drown.

Notice the last part of Proverbs 13:12, "...*but when the desire comes, it is a tree of life.*" When our expectations are met, we enjoy renewed energy and life invigorates us! We should capitalize on that renewed energy and use that moment to build up our faith for the future.

We can talk of hopes and dreams and goals, but unless we address the disappointment in our lives, we will carry it with us into the new goals or dreams the Holy Spirit is talking to us about, causing them to be flawed and weak.

The Elijah Syndrome

In 1 Kings 19, we read about Elijah's encounter with Ahab and his queen, Jezebel. Here's the scene leading up to this encounter:

While at Mount Carmel, Elijah came face to face with the prophets of Baal and experienced a supernatural victory. Fire from heaven came down, and God's power was displayed in many supernatural acts that went way beyond peoples' expectations. All of the prophets of Baal who were on that mountain were killed. Basically, it was the shootout at the O.K. Corral between Jehovah God and Baal to see who was the true God.

When the standoff was over, it was obvious to everyone, including Ahab, that Jehovah God was the real God. But Jezebel wouldn't accept that. In 1 Kings 19:1-2, we read:

> And Ahab told Jezebel all that Elijah had done, also how he had executed all the prophets with the sword. Then Jezebel sent a messenger to Elijah, saying, "So let the gods do to me, and more also, if I do not make your life as one of them by tomorrow about this time."

Right after this amazing victory for God, Elijah receives word that Jezebel is out to kill him.

Now remember that Elijah is the prophet who had just called fire down from heaven that consumed an altar made of water-soaked rock as well as the sacrifice on it. I would think that Elijah would be feeling on top of the world! But after hearing Jezebel's message to him, 1 Kings 19:3 says that Elijah, "...arose and ran for his life, and went to Beersheba...."

Elijah fled from the northern end all the way to the southern end of Israel. First Kings 19:4 says he:

...went a day's journey into the wilderness, and came and sat down under a broom tree. And he prayed that he might die, and said, "It is enough! Now, Lord, take my life, for I am no better than my fathers!"

That's what you call going from the top of the mountain to the bottom of the pit! Elijah moved from a place of victory to absolute defeat—wishing to die.

Notice the particular phrase Elijah spoke, "It is enough!" As mentioned previously, he'd had it. But there are some important distinctions to make if we are to really understand what *enough* means. Some people say Elijah reacted like he did because he was tired and spent. In fact, I've used this passage in the past to teach on fatigue and feeding yourself properly, spiritually or personally, when you need to rest.

Still, it's curious that Elijah reacts with such fear to one person threatening his life. You would think that no matter how fatigued he was, after seeing God's displays of power, Elijah would just ask God to finish the job and take care of Jezebel. Why do her words suddenly trump his faith? Well, I decided to do a little more research on the events leading up to this passage. Why the word *enough*?

In 1 Kings 17, God had sent Elijah to a widow. He said, *"Arise, go to Zarephath...and dwell there. See, I have commanded a widow there to provide for you."* Elijah arrives to find the widow is impoverished and has no food in the middle of a drought. I believe he is disappointed because, in his mind, this is not how God told him it would be. Elijah has to perform a miracle just so the barrel of meal and the flask of oil don't run out. He might have been thinking, *God, I thought You were sending me to a wealthy widow who could provide for me.*

We have all been there, when things did not turn out like we thought they should. Immediately disappointment sets in. Right then and there, you have to make a decision not to allow it to chip away at your faith. Elijah was facing the same thing. Soon after this provision miracle, the widow's son dies and Elijah has to perform a miracle to raise him back to life.

On the surface level, Elijah's reaction to Jezebel doesn't seem to make sense. He was having a revival for three years. Miracles were happening for him. Yes, he was fatigued, but why did he respond this way to Jezebel's threat? It is my belief that disappointing occurrences such as these set him up to react as he did to Jezebel. Despite all of the miracles God did through him, Elijah still had to deal with his unmet expectations. He had to wrestle with the knowledge that he was not in complete control. I believe that he was carrying those past disappointments with him. I call this "The Elijah Syndrome." There are many people today suffering with the same syndrome. They have been carrying disappointment with them for years.

Fatigue was definitely a factor for Elijah. But more than that, when the queen threatened him, it was a culmination of all of the evil tidings he had heard over the course of his life. Instead of his heart being established, he ran for his life and asked God to kill him.

Everyone can identify with Elijah because we have all lived with disappointment to some degree. You can receive endless teachings on faith and hear the Word over and over again, but if you allow a spirit of disappointment to rest on your life, then Satan can prevent you from living a full life of faith. Hebrews 4:2 says that the *"the gospel was preached to us as well as to them; but the word which they heard did not profit them, not being mixed with faith in those who heard it."* So it wasn't they didn't hear the Word, it is that their disappointment filtered out the Word that they heard and they received no benefit. It is vitally important that we recognize those disappointments and deal with them. Preferably, recognize and deal with disappointment when it first comes, so it doesn't defeat you.

Everyone Experiences Disappointment

Exodus 6:5-8 says:

> *And I have also heard the groaning of the children of Israel whom the Egyptians keep in bondage, and I have remembered My covenant. Therefore say to the children of Israel: "I am the Lord; I will bring you out from under the burdens of the Egyptians, I will rescue you from their bondage, and I will redeem you with an outstretched arm and with great judgments. I will take you as My people, and I will be your God. Then you shall know that I am the Lord your God who brings you out from under the burdens of the Egyptians. And I will bring you into the land which I swore to give to Abraham, Isaac, and Jacob; and I will give it to you as a heritage: I am the Lord."*

This is God Himself talking. He lists all these things that He is going to do for His children. What a promise! But verse 9 says, *"So Moses spoke thus to the children of Israel; but they did not heed Moses, **because of anguish of spirit and cruel bondage."***

In other words, they were despondent and discouraged because of a disappointed spirit. They were so consumed by their disappointment that even this powerful word from God did absolutely nothing for them. If we want to hear God's voice and receive His promises, we must let go of past disappointments.

I have observed some people who are in such deep depression that they can't really hear anything you say to them. Trying to cheer them up seems useless. You can be in the same situation when it comes to hearing God's voice. Because you are carrying those disappointments with you, they are all you can see and hear. They have been wearing away to make your heart sick, and as a result, you are not hearing what God is trying to say to you.

In 1 Samuel 1, the Bible says Hannah was heartbroken because she did not have a child. She began to literally cry out to God concerning her situation. Every time she would go to the temple, she would see mothers there, reminding her that she was barren. These reminders pressed on her disappointment of not having a child, causing Hannah even more anguish of spirit. As if that weren't enough, the taunting of her husband's other wife, who had children, deepened her grief.

Have you been there? Maybe you're having a bad time at your job or in some other area and other people or circumstances seem to rub it in even more? It just builds up. Satan uses those things to get us to carry disappointment with us. We don't set goals or see the future. But even worse than that, we don't hear the Word of the Lord that is coming forth.

Every person, young or old, must learn how to deal with disappointment. We will all encounter it, but how we deal with it determines whether or not we get sick with Elijah syndrome. Understanding disappointment and how it works in your life can be preventative medicine. You will know how to prevent your heart from becoming sick.

I've seen businesses, and even corporations, experience a disappointing result or event that affects their business and replaces the culture of vision with a culture of disappointment. Not only was the heart of an individual or many individuals sick, the heart of the organization was sick. I have also seen churches carry disappointments with them, even experiencing it in my own church life. I thank God that He gives us people who will come alongside us and give us a kick in the seat of the pants, spiritually speaking, to help us move beyond the disappointment. I hope that this chapter will serve as the kick in the seat of your spiritual pants!

We have to be extremely careful that we don't allow disappointment to dominate us, even in a corporate environment. Corporations, businesses, churches, and all organizations should celebrate when things start to happen and dreams and visions come to fruition. We must ensure that the expectations that we set are of God. There might be a temptation to run for the first positive thing that comes our way, but be patient. Just because it looks like Him, doesn't necessarily mean it is. He will answer the hopes and dreams He gave you in His own way, on His own timeline.

When those God-given expectations are finally met, rejoice! The celebration of met expectations is one of the greatest medicines you have against disappointment. Celebrating is moving forward in hope and faith for the future. Hope that is postponed makes the heart sick, but when the hope comes true, it is life-giving!

Hearing God's Voice

So what do we do when we encounter the inevitable frustration of disappointment? We can sit there and let our hearts be sick, or we can stand up and refuse to let it control us. Look at how these individuals in the Bible dealt with it.

In Exodus 6, God's direct word could not get through to the Israelites because of their anguished spirit. As we read previously, Hebrews 4:2 says, *"For indeed the gospel was preached to us as well as to them; but the word which they heard did not profit them, not being mixed with faith in those who heard it."* They were so caught up in dwelling on their disappointments, that they missed God's attempt to bless them!

Elijah essentially said, "I've had enough!" His frustrations were also a result of carrying disappointments with him. He had not taken the time to address those past disappointments until it reached a crisis point with Jezebel. *"It is enough!"* He knew something had to change.

Disappointment works like mineral spirits on varnished wood. It attacks your belief system and strips it away little by little. What was once there to protect you is slowly removed. When a spirit of disappointment fully operates in your life, it transforms into a spirit full of fear. When this happens, any bad tiding or negative comment or situation that comes our way overwhelms and defeats us. Disappointment has stripped our belief system, and like the stripped wood, we are left vulnerable and exposed, with nothing to protect us against fear and discouragement.

Philippians 3:13-14 (NIV) says:

> *Brothers and sisters, I do not consider myself yet to have taken hold of it. But one thing I do: Forgetting what is behind and straining toward what is ahead, **I press on** toward the goal **to win the prize** for which God has called me heavenward in Christ Jesus.*

The J.B. Phillips New Testament Bible version phrases it this way: "...I leave the past behind and with hands outstretched to whatever lies ahead I go straight for the goal—my reward the honour of being called by God in Christ."

Think about that picture. When we carry disappointments and allow them to consume our lives, we tend to put our hands in our pockets and look to the ground. We are not reaching out for the new things God has for us. Returning to 1 Kings, we see that God helped Elijah overcome his disappointment and reach out to the new by nourishing him with food and then giving him a deep sleep.

When disappointment is in your life, you have to be aware of it, and then you have to nourish yourself. After Elijah was nourished, the Bible says that God called him to come outside. Look at 1 Kings 19:11-12:

> *...And behold, the Lord passed by, and a great and strong wind tore into the mountains and broke the rocks in pieces*

before the Lord, but the Lord was not in the wind; and after the wind an earthquake, but the Lord was not in the earthquake; and after the earthquake a fire, but the Lord was not in the fire; and after the fire a still small voice.

Why would that happen? Why would God cause all these things and then not be in them?

I'll tell you why: Elijah thought that the only way he could hear from God was through the wind, the earthquake, or the fire. God was essentially saying, "If I'm going to take you out of your disappointment and take you to the next level, I need to communicate with you in a way that you've never been communicated with before. I'm going to change your situation, your mindset, and your environment."

I imagine Elijah was the sort of man who went big or went home. If there was going to be a miracle, he wanted fire to rain down. God wanted to show Elijah that He could do things different from what Elijah expected. The Word says that God spoke to Elijah in a still, small voice, and that he heard it. He caused Elijah to cross over from disappointment into faith.

With Elijah, God had always moved in ways that were similar to the wind or the fire or the earthquake. But suddenly, when God wanted to do something new, when He wanted to break Elijah out of the despair he was in, He appeared in a different way. God would not talk to Elijah about his future until he was prepared to let go of his past disappointment. God needed him to stop embracing the old disappointments so that he could turn and embrace what God had for him.

Sometimes we can't hear God's voice, just like the children of Israel in Exodus 6, because we are looking for God to always do things the way He's always done them. We want to put God in a box and say, "God, you're going to do it my way." But sometimes God moves in different ways in our lives so that we can hear what He's saying to us.

For some of us, all we are able to hear is our disappointments. But until you start listening to what God is saying, He won't speak to you about your life.

Letting Go of the Past

Paul talked in Philippians 3 of forgetting the things that are behind us. What he's describing is when you start feeling the pleasure of the future more than you feel the pain of the past. How do we forget the people who hurt and wrong us? You may not literally forget the act, but you will forget the pain because you get healed from the pain.

When you cling to that disappointment, though, the pain never heals. Some people are still feeling the pain five, ten, fifteen years after the incident. Here is the major issue—if you allow disappointment to stay that long, it actually becomes part of your belief system. It integrates itself into how you view life. It becomes a significant part of your perspective, your worldview. Some people have lived with disappointment so long that they don't notice it anymore! It leads them to expect disappointment. They think it's normal to feel that way.

When leaders allow this to happen, it can cause a variety of issues. One leader might try to do everything himself because he's experienced disappointment from people to whom he had entrusted tasks. Another might let things in her organization stagnate because she's allowing her own disappointments to cloud the future possibilities of her organization. Leadership is innately relational. It's your job to instill vision into the people you're leading. You can't do that if you allow disappointment to move your eyesight off of the future.

We need to forget the things that are behind us—forget the pain of the past and start reveling in the pleasure of the future. Celebrating the future is truly a step to closing the door on the past. Only when you close that door can you start pressing toward the new things God has for you.

I lived with a sinus infection for twenty years. I went to a family doctor, a specialist, and an allergist and had all three of them look at me. They told me I had one of the worst sinus infections they'd ever seen. I wasn't just experiencing symptoms when I was sick or had a cold. I was living with the painful symptoms every day of my life. The doctors asked me how long I'd been living with this condition and I didn't even know what they meant! I thought it was normal because I'd been living with it for years. They gave me medicine that helped and I felt like a new person!

Some of us have been living with the pressure of disappointment for so long it's become a way of life. We just deal with it. The Holy Spirit is saying, "I want to talk to you about a whole lot of things, but I can't because your head is plugged up. I want to show you what it's like to believe again, to dream again, and to hope again!"

Good things can happen for you in your life, if only you'll let go of past hurts and disappointments and reach with outstretched arms toward the future God has for you. You can overcome disappointment! And as a leader, the awesome thing is that you can then move forward to help others overcome disappointment as well.

Please pray this prayer with me: "God, help me to overcome disappointment. Help me to overcome the issues in my life that have kept me from hearing You. Open my heart to hear Your still, small voice. I'm sorry for putting You in a box and not letting You speak and work the way You want to. Help me to forget the disappointments I've held on to and reach with outstretched arms toward what's ahead. I want to forget the pain of the past and feel the pleasure of the future instead. Teach me to trust, to dream again, and to believe that You have a perfect plan for my life. Thank You that Your Holy Spirit's power has set me free from the chains and bondage of fear and disappointment. I choose to live my life in faith from this day forward. Amen."

CHAPTER 4

THE LEADER AND FAITH

Squeezing You into the World's Mold

The New Century Version of the Bible says in 1 John 5:1,4:

> *Everyone who believes that Jesus is the Christ is God's child, and whoever loves the Father also loves the Father's children. ...because **everyone who is a child of God conquers the world. And this is the victory that conquers the world—our faith.***

Ephesians 6:12 says:

> *For we do not wrestle against flesh and blood, but against principalities, against powers, against the rulers of the darkness of this age, against spiritual hosts of wickedness in the heavenly places.*

Those powers, rulers, and spiritual hosts refer to Satan and his followers. Until Jesus comes back, they have power in this world. And their main goal is to turn the world away from God. Their intention is to utilize the things in this world to disappoint you.

We can get hurt in the world's system and order every day. We were disappointed as a nation on 9/11/2001. We were disappointed as a community on April 20, 1999, here in Columbine, Colorado.

There are two words for *world* in the New Testament: *kosmos* and *aion*. The first refers to the world's order or system, while the second refers to an era or age. Specifically, *aion* is often associated with the evil spirit of this age before Christ's return. So not only will the world's system disappoint you with events that happen, but also people who operate in the spirit of this age who are influenced by Satan will disappoint you. Their deeds and actions can hurt. If you have a business relationship or you sign a contract with someone and they turn on you, lie about things, or do not do what they agreed to, they are being influenced by the spirit of this age. The enemy wants to work all these things to harm you.

On the other hand, *"we know that **all** things work together for good to those who love God…"* (Romans 8:28). He is a covenant God. He's not a man—He does not lie. God can always be counted on.

In the world, Satan will do everything he can to make sure you're disappointed. Satan's goal through the system of the world is to cause you to carry disappointment so that you turn away from God.

God's system in the Spirit is to get us to walk in faith. Hebrews 11:6 (NIV) says, *"Without faith it is impossible to please God…."* Now how does that work? Well, faith and disappointment are exactly the opposite.

If I carry disappointment in my life, it steals my faith. But if I walk in faith, faith will overcome the disappointment in my life. As a leader, it's your job to walk in faith and encourage those around you to do the same. You are tasked with instilling faith in others.

Romans 12:2 says, *"And do not be conformed to this world, but be transformed by the renewing of your mind, that you may prove what is that good and acceptable and perfect will of God."*

The J.B. Phillips translation of Romans 12:2 says:

> *Don't let the world around you squeeze you into its own mould, but let God re-mould your minds from within, so that you may prove in practice that the plan of God for you is good, meets all his demands and moves towards the goal of true maturity.*

One Christmas, back when my kids were in college, we had quite the hassle figuring out how to host our family coming in from out of town. We put the extended family in a downstairs suite that had all the accommodations to make them comfortable. But then there would no longer be space for our two children coming home from college. This is because my wife and I had gradually taken over the other bedrooms while they were gone! We turned one room into a huge closet, another into an exercise room, and another into a travel room.

I said, "Honey, we have five bedrooms and four bathrooms. How is it then that my kids are coming home from college and I don't have anywhere to put them?"

"I'll tell you what we do," she said. "We put them on the floor!"

So we bought air mattresses and put them in two of the bedrooms that we were using for other purposes.

After Christmas, as we were cleaning up, I had the joyful task of letting the air out of the mattresses. This was before the era of self-deflatable air mattresses! Have you ever tried to get the air out of one of those things? Well, it seemed it was taking me forever to finish this chore. There I was on top of that mattress trying to squeeze every bit of air out of it. It took me about an hour, but I finally got both deflated, folded, wrapped up, and placed back where they needed to be.

I learned something from that chore, because God can teach us lessons in the midst of any scenario. The world, this cosmos, is on you in the same way—trying to squeeze the air out of you. Some people have a big exit valve because of a history of disappointments. As soon as the world starts squeezing, all of their faith air whooshes out of them. The world tries to squeeze your faith out of you.

However, if you have a slow exit valve and a pump—which is the Word of God—being constantly pumped into your spirit, then you are set up for success. At the same moment that the world is squeezing you, the pump is pushing in even more air so that your faith doesn't falter. The faith air stays put and you get stronger all the time. You lose no faith, no air goes out. You are resisting the pressure of the world.

It would be like diving down deep in the ocean. The farther down you go, where the pressure is greater, the more you are squeezed. But there are vehicles that can actually go down several miles in the ocean. These vehicles are strong enough to withstand the water pressure of deep ocean. The Word of God within us makes us strong enough to withstand the world's pressure.

In this world there's a certain amount of pressure that Satan uses to bring disappointment to squeeze all of your faith in God out of you. He'll come after you to do that. But Paul says, *"Don't let the world around you squeeze you into its own mould."* Instead, he says, *"let God re-mould your minds from within."* In other words, when God brings the truth of the Word of God to you, those mattresses, spiritually speaking, get pumped up and you withstand the pressure that's trying to push everything out of you.

So, how are we going to overcome disappointment? By using the very opposite of disappointment, the victory that overcomes the world—faith!

Willing to Believe Again

In Mark 5:25-34, we can read a powerful story of faith. The situation for this particular woman looks grim: "Now a certain woman had a flow of blood for twelve years, and had suffered many things from many physicians. She had spent all that she had and was no better, but rather grew worse."

This woman was very sick, but after seeking help from doctor after doctor, she was broke and worse off than before. Chances are she was a woman of significant financial means since it took her twelve years to go broke. She went through the loss of her healthy physical body and her physical security. Crisis in those two areas will devastate anyone.

Her body had disappointed her. Doctors had disappointed her. Her bank account disappointed her. And the Scripture says nothing about how her family, marriage, and friends were affected by her sickness, but no doubt those aspects of her life suffered as well.

Despite all this, the Bible says that when this woman heard about Jesus, she came up behind Him in the crowd and touched His clothes: "For she said, 'If only I may touch His clothes, I shall be made well.'"

Some people who have experienced just one of these particular challenges would give up. Their past disappointments make them want to never try again. I've heard women say, "I'll never trust another man again." I've heard other people say, "I'll never work in a situation like that again." It's fine to decide that you are not going to do certain things again, especially if God was not in it to begin with.

But you cannot quit completely. It's not disappointment that defeats you; it's how you let the disappointment affect you on the inside that will crush you.

Now what jumps off the page at me is this: after twelve years of suffering, this woman hears of Jesus and is willing to step up to the plate and try again!

There were a lot of people around Jesus in this moment, touching Him and bumping into Him. In a crowd that size, chances are there was more than one sick, disappointed person. The Bible singles her out and says, "When she heard about Jesus." She evidently was the only one in the crowd willing to believe again in spite of her disappointments.

There are many people who have heard about Jesus, who have suffered many things, and are carrying disappointments but are not willing to believe again. This woman, though, did not let disappointment destroy her. She didn't allow her faith air to escape.

You can say, "Because of my failed marriage, I can never believe again." "Because my first business went bankrupt, I can never try again." It's understandable. But God is looking for spiritual antennas that will hook onto His Word. When the Word is preached, instead of having a downcast and disappointed spirit, be like this woman in Mark 5. When she heard of Jesus, her faith antenna immediately went up and she said, "I'm willing to believe one more time."

My church back in Louisiana had a member who was a self-made millionaire. I remember I once told him, "You know, for your age you seem to have had money for a long time."

"You don't really know my story do you?" he responded. "I was in business three other times before now. In each one of them, I had to file for bankruptcy. I went completely broke all three times."

I was shocked.

"By age 36, I had been bankrupt three times. I was broke. So I took a little 3x5 index card, clipped it on the bathroom mirror, and wrote, *Never Again.* I told myself, I'm not going to be broke ever again."

That man was willing to believe again. He was willing to step up to the plate one more time and swing the bat.

With all that she had been through, this woman in Mark 5 was willing to step up and try again; she was willing to believe again. The spirit of this age would tell us, "Don't step up and try again. Don't believe again. You're done, it's over."

When the woman heard of Jesus, she sought Him out. She didn't let disappointment dominate her life. She didn't let it get inside of her and destroy her faith. Instead, she said, "If only I may touch His clothes, I shall be made well." Let me tell you what—that's faith! What happened next?

> ***Immediately*** *the fountain of her blood was dried up, and she felt in her body that **she was healed of the affliction**. And Jesus, immediately knowing in Himself that power had gone out of Him, turned around in the crowd and said, "Who touched My clothes?" And He looked around to see her who had done this thing. But the woman, fearing and trembling, knowing what had happened to her, came and fell down before Him and told Him the whole truth.*

I think she took the time to tell Jesus what she had been through. The verse could have just said she told the truth, but instead the Bible emphasizes the *whole* truth. She told Him her whole story. After that, "*He said to her, 'Daughter, your faith has made you well. Go in peace, and be healed of your affliction.'*"

I believe the reason why Jesus said, "*Daughter, your faith has made you well*" was not simply because she touched Him in faith and power went out of Him and healed her. I believe what He was really saying is something like, *My goodness, look at everything this woman has gone through and yet she still stepped up to the plate in faith. She touched My garment in such a strength of faith that it drew power from Me that nobody else was tapping into.* So He said, "Daughter, *your faith* has made you well." He was speaking of more than just her action in that moment. He was speaking of how, despite everything she had suffered through, she still believed.

Faith in our lives is not automatic but disappointment is. If you live and breathe, you are going to experience disappointments from the world and experiences and other people. I know personally what it's like to *live* with a wounded, disappointed spirit. And I promise you there's not an ounce of faith within a hundred miles of a wounded, disappointed spirit. When you're wounded and carrying a disappointed spirit, you will have a hard time believing in anything, anybody, anywhere. You will be skeptical all the time. (There's a difference between wisdom and skepticism.) Some people live in that void and they never rise up.

Do not let disappointment dominate your life. Don't let it wound you and hold you back to the point where you can't rise up again and believe what God wants you to believe. People will live for years carrying disappointment with them because certain things didn't happen right in a relationship or in a business or their community or their church. They no longer reach out toward the future and they stop dreaming. Carrying disappointments with us robs us of our faith.

When Paul talked about forgetting the events of the past in Philippians 3, some people respond: "How do I forget the things that happened in the past? I've been disappointed in my life. I know I haven't forgotten the disappointment because I feel the pain of it. How do I know when I'm moving on?" Here's a clue. When you start feeling the anticipation of the future more than you do the pain of the past, you'll know that you're moving forward and out from under disappointment.

"And He said to her, 'Daughter, your faith has made you well.'" This woman's faith allowed her to again envision a future free of her symptoms. This woman suffered many things from many doctors. She was broke, and she was sick. All worldly signs said that she would be the last person in the crowd to touch Jesus with any ounce of faith. Yet, she touched Him and her willing heart caused Him to stop in His tracks.

Are you ready for this? To overcome disappointment, you have to be willing to try again. You must to be willing to believe again. You must be willing to dream again.

Defeating the Spirit of Disappointment

So how do you defeat the spirit of disappointment? Nahum 1:9 says, "What do you conspire against the Lord? He will make an utter end of it. Affliction will not rise up a second time."

This verse states what our goal is regarding disappointment—to bring it to an utter end so that it will not rise up a second time. Disappointments in life will still occur; however, you do not have to succumb to a spirit of disappointment ever again. The following are steps to help you completely defeat the spirit of disappointment.

- *Recognize it.* The prodigal son (see Luke 15:11-32) was not capable of turning his life around until he "came to himself." While he was in the pig pen he asked himself, "How many of my father's servants have food to eat?" Once he "came to himself," he quickly concluded that his father's servants were in much better condition than he was. This recognition began his road to restoration and taking his rightful place at his father's side.

- *Know that it is common.* First Peter 5:8-9 says, "Be sober, be vigilant; because your adversary the devil walks about like a roaring lion, seeking whom he may devour. Resist him, steadfast in the faith, knowing that the same sufferings are experienced by your brotherhood in the world." Disappointment is experienced by all of us at one time or another. First Peter says, "...knowing that the same sufferings are experienced by your brotherhood in the world." One of the greatest lies that we believe is that we are the only one going through what we are experiencing—but the fact is that many people around us are battling the same kinds of things.

- *Don't panic.* Become a problem solver. Turn lemons into lemonade. Many times when we panic it is an overreaction to something that has happened. Instead of seeing a solution to the problem, we magnify it to the point that we become paralyzed. The problem grows even bigger and we slip into deeper disappointment. If you feel yourself panicking whenever the unexpected happens, ask yourself these questions:

  » Am I seeing the problem accurately?

  » Have I verified my impression of the problem with others?

  » Have I identified at least two approaches to solving the problem?

  » Have I spoken with others who have gone through

similar situations?

» Is my pride hindering me in finding a solution?

- *Do not dwell on "What If's."* Do not become trapped in self-pity. Helen Keller said, "Self-pity is our worst enemy and, if we yield to it, we can never do anything wise in this world." The flow of wisdom and creativity is stopped in our lives when we build a dam of self-pity. Nothing in life moves ahead while dwelling on what might have been.

- *Assume a blessing is being disguised as a problem.* In 1856, a Frenchman was vacationing in Egypt and fell in love with that distant and fascinating country that straddles the Nile. Everything that he saw was immense and imposing. While in Egypt, he met another countryman, Ferdinand de Lesseps. De Lesseps was a dreamer on a grand scale. He wanted to connect the Mediterranean Sea with the Red Sea by a canal. In response, the other Frenchman also yearned to create something monumental.

By 1859, de Lesseps had been granted approval for his task of building the Suez Canal. The first Frenchman decided that he would build a lighthouse twice the size of the Sphinx for the entrance of the canal. His lighthouse would be a signal flooding light upon Egypt's present greatness and its past grandeur. All would clearly see the cultural eminence of Egypt with his beacon. He spent several years designing the project during which he created a lot of enthusiasm among Egyptians and others. However, the money was not forthcoming to build his colossus of a woman with an outstretched arm pointing a torch to the heavens so that all could see her light. Disappointed, he returned to France.

Back home, the dreamer of greatness soon found a harbor and home for his Suez Canal lighthouse. In 1875, the actual construction began in France. However, it wasn't long before Auguste Bartholdi's sculpture graced another harbor; this harbor was worlds away from the intended original home in Egypt. Bartholdi's colossus became a gift of the French government on the centennial of the United States of America. The Statue of Liberty is indeed a colossus standing over 150 feet tall and weighing nearly a half million pounds. At her base is inscribed Emma Lazarus' words:

> *Give me your tired, your poor,*
> *Your huddled masses yearning to breathe free,*
> *The wretched refuse of your teeming shore.*
> *Send these, the homeless, tempest-tost to me:*
> *I lift my lamp beside the golden door!*

Lazarus' words apply also to each resident of this land of the free. The Statue of Liberty lifts her torch not just to huddled masses to see freedom, but she can lighten our lives with this reminder that disappointments can be turned, with determination, into successes.

- Allow yourself to grieve. Whenever disappointment does occur, give yourself the time to process it emotionally and spiritually.

- Don't be eager to make new plans, change jobs, or cut off relationships.

- Don't lay the blame entirely on the other person.

- Don't lash out and try and inflict pain as revenge.

- Don't say "I don't care" when you really do.

- Don't assume that you know the whole truth behind what happened.

- Don't allow disappointment to develop into bitterness.

- Do ask questions and try and understand the situation better.

- Do examine your actions and see if you contributed in any way.

- Do talk it over with a friend or counselor.

- Do offer forgiveness even if it is not warranted.

- Do abandon foolish expectations.

Many years ago, I had to deal with a lady who was expecting God to give her a married minister as her new husband. When I questioned her about it, it was clear that she had dreamed up this foolish expectation. When I explained to her that this minister was very happy in his marriage and that his wife was quite unhappy about her pursuit, she would not listen to anything that I had to say. She became deeply disappointed when the minister and his wife met with her and explained that what she was expecting was not going to happen.

Whenever we have unrealistic expectations, we will always be disappointed.

- ***Be willing to risk again.*** Please carefully read the following quote by Helen Keller: "Security is mostly a superstition. It does not exist in nature, nor do the children of men as a whole experience it. Avoiding danger is no safer in the long run than outright exposure. Life is either a daring adventure or nothing." Someone said, "Life is risky. You are not going to get out alive." In other words, risk is an everyday part of life. Disappointment happens, but we should not be afraid to dream again and hope again.

- **Protect your heart against disappointment.** It is possible to prevent your heart from ever developing a disappointed spirit. Matthew 15:21-28 says, *"Then Jesus went out from there and departed to the region of Tyre and Sidon. And behold, a woman of Canaan came from that region and cried out to Him, saying, 'Have mercy on me, O Lord, Son of David! My daughter is severely demon-possessed.' But He answered her not a word. And His disciples came and urged Him, saying, 'Send her away, for she cries out after us.' But He answered and said, 'I was not sent except to the lost sheep of the house of Israel.' Then she came and worshiped Him, saying, 'Lord, help me!' But He answered and said, 'It is not good to take the children's bread and throw it to the little dogs.' And she said, 'Yes, Lord, yet even the little dogs eat the crumbs which fall from their masters' table.' Then Jesus answered and said to her, 'O woman, great is your faith! Let it be to you as you desire.' And her daughter was healed from that very hour."*

This dear lady is an excellent example for us. When she came to Jesus and asked Him to help her daughter, the Bible says that Jesus did not even acknowledge her. Then when she asked for help again, He told her that she was not good enough. Most of us would have been done pursuing Him at the time He did not acknowledge us. However, she cried after the second rejection, *"Lord help me…."* Then Jesus called her a dog and she responded, *"Yes, Lord, yet even the little dogs eat the crumbs from their masters' table."* WOW! This mother never had to overcome a spirit of disappointment because she never got disappointed to begin with. Let it be so with you and me as well.

CHAPTER 5

THE LEADER AND CHANGE

Innovation in Your Life

In the business world, there are disruptive innovations that change the story or paradigm. Cellular technology was one such innovation that disrupted how we communicated. It displaced older technology, changed how we viewed communication, and created a new market.

Behind the success of every innovation is something powerful—determination. Someone, somewhere has an idea that the person knows will change how things work. But his or her determination to see it through is what brings that innovation to life!

The strongest power in your life is the power of your will. If you do not like the direction your life is headed, you can choose to disrupt it. Just as God sat on the edge of a universe that was empty and void and chose to disrupt it with the creation of the sun, moon, planets, and stars, we can also choose to disrupt the nothingness in our lives. You can disrupt depression. You can disrupt inadequate feelings. You can disrupt financial and relational challenges. When you decide to disrupt something in your life, you do more than hope that things will get better; you choose to change them. This is innovation in your life.

Many people feel stuck in their jobs. But guess what—they, and you, can decide to change jobs! You are never stuck. Yes, it might be a long and slow process to find a new job, but it is possible. You can do anything you want to do, even if it's wrong. God gave us the power of choice way back in the Garden. He respects our power of choice because that power is what makes us most like Him. It is up to us to exercise that power and choose good things.

> Then He spoke a parable to them: "No one puts a piece from a new garment on an old one; otherwise the new makes a tear, and also the piece that was taken out of the new does not match the old. And no one puts new wine into old wineskins; or else the new wine will burst the wineskins and be spilled, and the wineskins will be ruined. But new wine must be put into new wineskins, and both are preserved. And no one, having drunk old wine, immediately desires new; for he says, 'The old is better'" (Luke 5:36-39).

When there is new wine, we must offer God a new wineskin. This new wineskin we offer God is a renewed mind. We must have a spirit that is ready to change.

Change Is Inevitable

Change, both good and bad, happens to everyone. You cannot escape change. In fact, the only thing that really remains the same is change itself! Change is the essence of life. It is constant. Our world is in perpetual motion. Summer will become fall. Water will wear down rock. Buildings will be replaced. Shoes will be replaced. We are constantly moving forward or going backward; there is no such thing as standing still. With that in mind, how do we ensure that we keep moving forward?

The Bible commands us to change, but did you know it also tells us how to change? Romans 12:2 is the call-to-change Scripture. The entire process of change can be encapsulated in this one verse mentioned a few times previously: *"And do not be conformed to this world, but be transformed by the renewing of your mind...."*

In the original language, the word *transformed* actually means changed. It is the same word used to describe the metamorphosis of a caterpillar into a butterfly. The word *renew* also means to change. With these definitions, we could rewrite the verse like this: "And do not be conformed to this world, but be changed by changing your mind."

The word *transformed* also implies a transition. Many people try to take one giant step to go from where they currently are to where they want to be. Then when they trip and fall, they don't understand why. They wouldn't be confused, though, if they had a good understanding of the nature of change.

There are two types of change: forced and proactive. Forced changes come when external events you do not initiate happen to you. Proactive changes are changes you choose to make to improve the quality of your life.

Changing Beliefs

To renovate an old house, you need a plan, and you need to gather your tools. You start work by taking out the old to make room for the new. You knock down a wall or tear out a sink or rip out old carpet. Once the old is gone, you can start implementing the new as you hang new sheetrock, apply fresh paint, and do whatever finishing touches it takes to make things look perfect. With a few tools, some supplies, and lots of time and effort, you can transform the place into something new and charming. Renovation is hard work, but if you want change badly enough, it is achievable.

Romans 12:2 says to be *"transformed by the renewing of your mind."* *To renew* means *to change* and *to renovate.* Renovation always begins with tearing down the old. As we renovate our minds, we tear down old, crippling beliefs and make room for new productive beliefs.

God gives us the spiritual tools necessary for mind renovation. In 2 Corinthians 10:4 we read, *"For the weapons of our warfare are not carnal but mighty in God for pulling down strongholds."* The phrase "pulling down" means *demolition.* What do we need to demolish? What do we have to renovate? What is it about our minds that needs to be changed? We need to change the crippling beliefs that have formed strongholds in our minds!

Demolition and Renovation

The word *stronghold* refers to a castle or a fortress. Right now, there are castles and fortresses in your mind that need to be demolished or renovated. They are built out of crippling beliefs that have formed over a period of years. Wrong beliefs about God, yourself, or circumstances in your life hurt you and hinder your progress toward change. If you want to experience positive change, you must start by demolishing untrue belief strongholds. They are preventing you from achieving your dreams and desires.

Some of your strongholds are built out of good beliefs. When you stand strong in a conviction, that is coming from a stronghold, a mental fortress you have built to protect that belief. The problem arises when the belief you are protecting is false, like the belief that you are worthless or a failure. These are the kinds of strongholds that must be torn down and replaced with fortresses of empowering beliefs.

Your mind is made up of your thoughts, your feelings, and your beliefs. These three work together to affect your behavior. Your behavior, in turn, determines the results you get in life. If you do not like the results you are getting, you need to change your behavior, but your behavior will not truly change until you change your beliefs. This is why all permanent change begins in the mind.

Understanding Beliefs

Because changing your beliefs is directly connected to changing your behavior, it is important to understand how beliefs are formed. Remember this simple formula: Your thoughts + your feelings = your beliefs.

The closest most people come to experiencing faith is fear. Fear is visceral. Your thoughts and feelings take you to a place where you believe what you fear is true. You experience the sensations of fear in sight, sound, and feeling. We experience fear this way even if the fear is completely irrational.

Faith works in exactly the same way; it just requires more work on your part. You need to create thoughts and feelings that will make you believe what you are having faith for is true. Faith is experiencing the sight, sound, and feeling of things for which you are believing. Even when it is irrational, faith believes so deeply that you can actually feel the reality of what you are believing.

Faith is a conviction of the truth about anything. You can have faith in the wrong things and be convinced those things are true when they are in fact not! Some people believe wrong things about themselves, about their marriages, their past, their finances, or even about their God. They experience physical sensations of those wrong beliefs. If you simply believe that the bogeyman is real, he can make goose bumps come up all over your arms.

Let's take the example of someone who was abused as a child by an authority figure. From that abuse, he formed the false, crippling belief that there are no loving or caring authority figures. As an adult, he now has problems relating to his boss, pastor, police officers, the IRS, and anyone who tries to tell him what to do. That is the result of a hindering belief. A stronghold has developed in his mind.

The sad part is that many of us are not even aware we have hindering beliefs. We continue to live as though they are true when they aren't. We do things a certain way, give certain responses, and continue to function in life at a level much lower than our potential because of these hindering beliefs.

Demolition of Despair

I once went through a very trying personal experience in which I had to demolish some hindering beliefs that were causing me to be severely depressed. It started when some people dealt dishonestly with me, causing me to lose several hundred thousand dollars. The resulting depression almost killed me.

During this time, a close friend tried to encourage me, but I was in such a place of despair that I resisted all his efforts to help. He wanted to help me change my emotional and spiritual environment by praying with me, but I was in no mood for prayer. I was looking for an easy way out of my dilemma, but there were some personal adjustments I needed to make. He kindly, but firmly, told me I had to change my mental focus. He insisted that I start praying for those who had wronged me so severely.

That was not easy. But as I started to follow his suggestion—or more accurately, the biblical order—the grip of depression started to loosen. As I changed my mental focus and my behavior, I began to feel free of the despair and depression that was crippling me.

Then my friend told me something that really changed my focus. He told me that all the money that had been taken from me was going to come back to me! I had a very difficult time believing him. Nevertheless, within minutes of him telling me this, a man knocked on my office door and handed me what I thought was an appreciation card. Upon closer inspection, however, I realized it was a check for fifty thousand dollars! Now my crippling beliefs were being challenged in a big way!

Within one month, I saw a total of $130,000 returned, and all the legal issues I had been fighting for three years were resolved. My disabling beliefs were totally blown right out of my mind.

Examples of Crippling Beliefs

In order to demolish these strongholds, you must first identify your wrong beliefs such as: *God doesn't love me. I'm not good enough. Everyone is laughing at me.* These are just a few examples of hindering beliefs people have.

If you want to change your life, the first task is to identify any beliefs that have kept you bound to your current condition. You may believe that you get sick easily or that nobody likes you. There are women who believe all men are egotistic, and men who believe all women are nags. These beliefs bind people to negative conditions.

Thoughts plus feelings equal your beliefs. Your beliefs affect your behavior. Your behavior determines the results you get in life. Every negative behavior you have is directly connected to a crippling belief.

The first step toward changing your behavior is to change your hindering beliefs. In order to change them, you must first identify them.

Emotional Resistance

Hindering beliefs show up as emotional resistance. You know you are facing emotional resistance when images and thoughts that directly contradict the changes you want to make appear in your mind. For instance, you begin a new diet and vivid images of lemon pie or cheesecake keep coming into your mind. Like a magnet, hindering beliefs will pull you back to what is comfortable and familiar—and not always healthy.

Many people falsely think that if they were supposed to change, they would feel better about it. But that is not true. The initial resistance you feel toward change is driven by your negative emotions, which are directly connected to wrong beliefs. As you take action to change, your emotions and your hindering beliefs will try to convince you that you're headed in the wrong direction. But as you build new, empowering beliefs in your life, your positive emotions will aid you.

Remember my friend who challenged me to pray for those who had taken money from me? In order to get me to pray for them, he practically carried me into their business place! I had such strong feelings of hostility toward those people that it would be a vast understatement to say I felt emotional resistance. As I willfully began to focus on blessing them, however, something unusual began to happen. My focus changed, my beliefs about them changed, and the anger and disappointment I was experiencing began to leave. I persevered through the emotional resistance and actually underwent a significant transformation in my attitude toward them.

Every change begins with an ending. It is impossible to embrace something new if you are still holding onto the old. If I am hugging one person, I must let that person go before I can hug another. When we become aware of the hindering beliefs in our lives and let them go, we are free to embrace new, beneficial beliefs that will empower us for positive, permanent change.

Changing Emotions

One of the keys to success in life is intelligent management of emotions. Emotions were created by God, but how you manage them determines whether they serve you positively or negatively. Positive emotions infuse passion and vitality into our everyday lives. They give us the energy to do the things we need to do. Negative emotions, on the other hand, hinder our progress toward our goals. They can paralyze us from taking action to solve our problems.

God is interested in you as a whole person. Positive emotions promote positive actions. Negative emotions promote negative actions or sometimes prevent action. If you allow the Holy Spirit to help you replace negative emotional patterns with positive emotional patterns, you will find yourself empowered to rise up and remain faithful to the purpose He has called you to fulfill.

Let's revisit Elijah in 1 Kings 19.

Elijah had just challenged the 450 prophets of Baal to a duel and won. God came through, sending fire from heaven, and not one person who worshiped the false god escaped. It was an impressive show of God's power and Elijah's faith.

But, in the middle of his victory, Elijah received a murderous threat from Queen Jezebel that completely altered his emotional condition. Jezebel, irate that her prophets were destroyed, sent Elijah a message that she was coming after him and was going to kill him.

Elijah had taken down 450 of her prophets, and she still wouldn't give up! Receiving this threat changed Elijah from rejoicing in one moment to wanting to die in the next. His emotional condition changed in a second!

An angel came and ministered to Elijah, then Elijah set off on a forty-day trip to Mount Horeb where he hid himself in a cave. While he was there, God began to ask him some questions.

When God asked Elijah what he was doing in the cave, Elijah poured out his negative emotions. He complained that even though he had done a good thing in killing the false prophets, now Jezebel was after him. He also lamented the fact that he was the only one left serving God.

Elijah experienced two primary negative emotions here—fear and loneliness—and God immediately dealt with both. First, He dealt with Elijah's fear by showing him that He had a plan to protect him. Then He dealt with the loneliness issue by informing Elijah that there were actually seven thousand other God-followers of whom Elijah was not aware. His fear and loneliness were taken care of, so Elijah left the cave behind and followed the instructions God had given him.

If God had not dealt with the emotions that were troubling Elijah, he would have continued to overreact and magnify the situation. His negative emotions would have paralyzed him. But Elijah did what God commanded him to do, and because of that obedience, his life was changed. Jezebel eventually met her doom and Elijah was safe and no longer alone. He was able to take positive action because God helped him manage his negative emotions intelligently.

In Elijah's case, God was able to get his attention and the negative emotions were dispatched fairly quickly. But sometimes the healing process is not so quick or easy. Thankfully, there are a handful of things you can do to manage your emotions.

Managing Your Emotions

1. Avoid overreacting. When a challenge comes, a negative event occurs, or someone criticizes us, most people tend to overreact. Elijah allowed the whole situation with Queen Jezebel to get blown out of proportion. Sometimes, we attach the wrong meaning to events in our lives. Suppose a driver pulls his car out in front of your car. You honk the horn at him, feeling justified because he did something wrong. Later, you find out he was rushing his young child to the hospital. Now you feel guilty for honking! The event is the same, but now you have attached a different meaning to it. Thankfully, you have the ability to intentionally infuse meaning into events. The next time someone pulls out in front of you, you can choose to react appropriately. You can think, *I'm not going to honk. I'm not going to overreact. I refuse to attach negative meaning to this situation.*

2. Size up your situation. Look at the facts realistically and rationally, without assuming any motives or meanings. Asking yourself the right questions will help you do this: *What will it matter two hundred years from now? Is this really the way it is, or am I blowing things out of proportion?* Try to detach yourself from the emotions and see the situation objectively. Sometimes you are too close to a situation to see it clearly. It's important to bring in other voices to help you clarify things. I usually ask my wife, "Am I seeing this clearly?" Her view helps me put things into proper perspective. More importantly, let God speak to you about the situation. A simple prayer can work wonders, "Lord, help me to see this situation through Your eyes and not the eyes of my emotions." He can put your circumstances into perspective for you, just as He did for Elijah.

3. *Do not deny negative emotions.* When you deny that a situation is happening, it's like an ostrich sticking its head in the sand, pretending that the predator doesn't exist. Sometimes we stick our heads in metaphorical sand and pretend that our situation does not exist or that it does not bother us. You shouldn't magnify your emotions, but you cannot ignore them either. If you have a troubled teenager, you are going through a financial crisis, experiencing marital problems, or going through some other dark time, you are probably feeling a lot of fear. This fear can cause you to shut down emotionally. Denial can prevent you from taking actions that will bring about positive change. It's important to acknowledge and process your emotions. That is the only way to move past them.

4. *Respond correctly.* When God spoke to Elijah, He dealt very specifically with Elijah's negative emotions. God gave Elijah a specific action to take to overcome those feelings. The primary negative emotions most people have are fear, anger, disappointment, guilt, depression, and inadequacy. Identify what negative feelings you are most vulnerable to. Ask questions until you get to the root of the belief that is causing that emotion. Then, whenever that emotion pops up, attack it with truth. If you struggle with fear, chant Psalm 56:3, *"Whenever I am afraid, I will trust in You."* If you struggle with inadequacy or confidence, say Philippians 4:13 aloud: *"I can do all things through Christ who strengthens me."* When negative emotions arise, confront them with the truth, don't stuff them away. Remind yourself of past successes and don't dwell on past failures. If you expect failure, then trust me, you will encounter it. If you practice developing healthy mental patterns now, you will one day find you are master of your mind.

5. *Learn from your negative emotions.* Negative emotions always point to something deeper like your hidden, false beliefs. That feeling of inadequacy is not random; it is birthed from a false belief that was probably birthed in a painful moment in your past. Maybe you feel lonely or unlikeable. When you prod those feelings, you might find yourself remembering the last time you felt that way. Negative emotions can also point to wrong behavior. God twice asked Elijah, *"What are you doing here?"* God knew there was something wrong in Elijah's life, and by asking that question, He sought to open Elijah's eyes to that fact. Elijah's negative emotions of fear and loneliness had paralyzed him from making any further progress toward his goals. He was too busy hiding! God challenged him to go and do the things he needed to do. Similarly, we need to be challenged to learn from our emotions and tackle our problems head-on.

6. Change things up. There are two primary ways you can change your emotions. First, you can change your focus. If you are experiencing fear, it is because you are focusing on mental pictures that bring fear. So change the mental picture. Ask the Holy Spirit to give you a positive image to replace your negative one. Every time a fearful thought enters your mind, imagine batting it away and pulling up a new, hopeful image. Eventually, this will become second nature. The second way you can change your emotions is by changing your actions. Positive actions can inspire positive emotions. If a couple wants to feel romance again, they need to start taking romantic actions: go on dates, write poetry, sacrifice for each other in little ways. The romantic feelings will follow the actions. Negative emotions can feel overwhelming. But with a committed mental effort, you can change your focus and actions and take control of your emotions.

7. Use your positive emotions as motivators. When a *positive* emotion strikes you, take hold of it and seize the day. Your positive emotions can give you a boost to tackle change. But you don't have to sit and wait for positive emotions to come your way! Ask the Lord to fill you with positive emotions, specifically the fruit of the Spirit: *"But the fruit of the Spirit is love, joy, peace, longsuffering, kindness, goodness, faithfulness, gentleness, self-control"* (Galatians 5:22-23). Most fruit on that list can be both an emotion and a behavior. Love is an emotion, but it is also an action. The fruit of the Spirit are expressed inwardly as our emotions and outwardly as our actions. These positive emotions can empower you to reach your dreams, treat others with compassion, and to see life in positive terms. Focusing on and practicing the fruit of the Spirit can keep negative emotions at bay. Practice them every day—both internally and externally.

Emotions are a gift from God, but they are meant to be intelligently managed—not manage us! Even when faced with the fear of death, Jesus obeyed and took control of His emotions. His negative emotions spoke fear into His life (Mark 14:36; Luke 22:42). His positive emotions spoke love, and so He saved the world.

Develop a Change Strategy

Through wisdom a house is built, and by understanding it is established; by knowledge the rooms are filled with all precious and pleasant riches (Proverbs 24:3-4).

If you really want to change, you must develop a strategy.

Proverbs 24:3-4 tells us that with a strategy, we can build our dream house of positive change. Having a strategy is like having a road map. If you take a trip without a map, you can easily get off course. With a map, however, it's easy to find the way to where you want to go.

What is the main reason people abort their progress toward change? They face resistance. They begin to feel badly or uncomfortable during the process of change, so they just give up. But if you take the time to develop a strategy, that strategy will become the map to help you maneuver past any resistance.

The following is an eight-step plan to developing a strong strategy for change:

Step One: Expose Yourself to a New Environment

The first step toward developing a strategy for change is to expose yourself to a new environment. One of the best ways to jump-start change is to interrupt your normal patterns. You need exposure to something different.

Maybe your daily life has become monotonous. You get up, eat breakfast, drink coffee, go to work, come home, watch a little TV, and go to bed. Then, repeat. In order for you to experience change, your daily rhythm needs to be interrupted. Now this does not require you to make a radical change; even something as simple as exercising for thirty minutes a day or reading something positive and inspirational every morning will make a tremendous difference.

In Acts 9, Saul, who persecuted Christians, experienced a major life interruption. He was on his regular course of business when God showed up in the form of a bright light and knocked him off his horse. When Saul hit the dirt, the first word out of his mouth was "Lord." That was a major change in routine! He went from persecuting Christians to calling Jesus "Lord" in a matter of seconds. God needed to interrupt his daily pattern a bit more though, so He blinded Saul for three days. Saul stepped up to the challenge and eventually became the man we know as Paul.

If you are having trouble with your marriage, plan a bi-weekly dinner date with a couple whose marriage you admire. Their influence will rub off on you and your spouse. If you are dissatisfied with your job, hang out with people who are enjoying fulfilling careers. Discover what they are thinking, seeing, and expecting. Fill your mind with new information. You must learn to see differently, hear differently, and even smell differently if you want to experience change. A new environment will help you do just that.

Step Two: Locate and Use Available Resources

The second step toward developing a strategy for change is to locate and use the resources that are available to you. When Nehemiah wanted to rebuild the walls of Jerusalem, he went to the greatest resource he had—the king (Nehemiah 2). With the king's help, Nehemiah was able to accomplish his goal.

There are many resources available to help anyone change, but most people never take the time to do a little digging and find, let alone use, these resources. Books, audiobooks, social media, podcasts, blogs, vlogs, programs, groups, magazines—these are just a few of the resources out there that are easy to find and generally free to access. There is a wealth of information available that can teach you how to improve any area of your life. If you're trying to lose weight on a budget, try renting a workout DVD at the library or following a fitness blogger. There are lots of options for you, no matter your age or technological savvy.

Things will snowball for you if you just get out there and look.

Step Three: Find Someone to Coach You

The third step toward developing a strategy for change is to find what may be the most important resource you can have—someone who will coach you. This person will be your moral support when the going gets tough. A coach can provide you with the wisdom of experience and give you encouragement and advice. This could be a friend or a relative, even a coworker or boss, if the situation is appropriate. It could be your pastor, your small group leader, or just an acquaintance.

The point is to be bold in asking for help. If you want to lose weight and know someone who is at the gym constantly, ask if you can tag along! If you want to climb the ladder at work and you have a successful colleague, ask if you can learn from him or her.

If you cannot find someone who is willing to coach you in person, all is not lost. Find someone you admire and get your hands on all the content they produce: their blog, book, program, etc. As busy as I now am in my daily life, I'm not always able to meet in person with a mentor. Now, if I want to learn something, I pick a guru to follow online and devour the content. Finding people you can pattern your success after is a shortcut to change.

Step Four: Imagine the Pain

This might sound strange, but it's important to really imagine the pain you will experience by staying the same. Picture it in detail—sight, sound, and feeling. Imagine your health's trajectory if you stay the same. Imagine the unhappiness you feel in your job every day. I know this is not a fun task, but it is a motivating one. The Bible tells us in 2 Corinthians 7:10, *"Godly sorrow produces repentance leading to salvation."* The word *sorrow* means pain, and the word *repentance* means to change your mind. So, another translation of that passage could read, "The pain that you allow God to direct leads to a changing of the mind."

Whenever you connect your current behavior to pain, you become willing to let go of that behavior and embrace change. If you tell a child not to touch a hot stove but the youngster does it anyway, chances are you will never have to warn that child again. The sight of the stove will be a reminder of the pain, and it will be avoided.

Ask yourself the following questions to help you imagine that pain of not changing your mind:

- What short-term consequences will I suffer if I don't change?

- What long-term consequences will be the result of staying the same?

- If I don't change, how will staying the same affect my family and friends?

- What creative methods can I use to make myself aware of these consequences?

Fear alone will not change you. But if you harness your fear rightly and combine it with hope, it can motivate you.

Step Five: Imagine the Gain

The fifth step is the opposite of the fourth. Instead of picturing the pain you will suffer as a result of not changing, picture the benefits you will experience if you do change. Again, imagine this in vivid detail—sight, sound, and feeling. Most people do this automatically when they decide to change from being single to being married. They daydream of the intimacy and companionship they will experience in marriage. Perhaps you daydream of the joy you will have when you change from being stressed about finances to being in control of your finances. Think about your favorite benefits of changing and hold tightly to them.

Ask yourself a few questions to form your mental picture of your life after change:

- What short-term benefits will I experience if I change?

- What long-term benefits will be the result of my changing?

- If I change, will that change affect my family and friends?

- What creative ways can I use to make myself aware of these benefits?

Step Six: Determine How You Will Deal with Resistance

The next step you must take in developing your change strategy is determining how you will deal with emotional resistance. When you start down the road to change, you will encounter resistance, and it won't just be internal resistance. Yes, if you decide to go on a diet, images of cheesecake will inevitably appear in your mind. But you'll also experience the outside pressure of friends saying, "Come on, just cheat this once!" Your emotions and, unfortunately, sometimes your environment will violently resist the change. Many people give up when the resistance gets tough, but that's when you need to get tougher.

The path to dealing with resistance is not uniform because we are all different and our communities are different. So think carefully about your life and potential triggers. Plan out how you will act and what you will say when faced with resistance. Overcome your feelings of guilt brought on by past failures, and focus instead on the things you have accomplished. Don't focus on the places you have fallen short. Just get up, and reimagine the gain.

Step Seven: Replace Harmful Thoughts and Behaviors with Beneficial Ones

A major key to assimilating a desired change into your life is to replace harmful thoughts and behaviors with those that are encouraging and beneficial. This is the substitution principle. Substitute something positive for something negative.

One of the reasons dieting is so difficult is because you cannot stop eating completely. The best option, then, is to replace fattening foods with healthy foods. I enjoy eating meat, so I replaced carb-heavy foods with protein-heavy foods. I was able to eliminate a familiar, damaging food pattern by replacing it with a beneficial one.

The same substitution principle applies to thoughts. If you struggle with a certain negative thought, replace it continually with a positive one until the new thought becomes a habit. This is where biblical confession can help. You can break negative thinking patterns by countering them with the Word of God. For example, every time you think, *I'm not going to make it,* replace this thought with Philippians 4:13: *"I can do all things through Christ who strengthens me."* Keep doing that until Philippians 4:13 flows naturally from your thoughts. Let that truth sink in. Believe me, there is a Bible verse that is perfect for whatever change you're attempting to assimilate.

Step Eight: Choose Your Reward

The last step you should take to prepare yourself for personal change is to decide how you will reward yourself for your accomplishment. In 1 Samuel 17:26, before David went out to fight Goliath, David asked, *"What shall be done for the man who kills this Philistine?"* I'm sure David was motivated purely to defend the honor of God Almighty! But the generous reward being offered by King Saul was a nice motivator. God understands the importance of rewards. In fact, Hebrews 11:6 tells us that He is a rewarder of those who seek Him.

Rewards may be something you desire or something you need. A two-week trip to Hawaii is a great reward for losing fifty pounds but so is the benefit of better health or the ability to finish a marathon. Use something important to you as motivation for personal change. Always think big when it comes to rewards!

Knowing in advance how you will reward yourself once the goal is reached enables you to overcome any short-term discomforts of change. You know your reward is waiting!

PART TWO

LEADERSHIP
AND OTHERS

CHAPTER 6

THE LEADER AND DISCIPLESHIP

Identifying and Developing Leaders

Isaiah 61:3 says:

> To console those who mourn in Zion, to give them beauty for ashes, the oil of joy for mourning, the garment of praise for the spirit of heaviness; that they may be called the trees of righteousness, **the planting of the Lord**, that He may be glorified.

I want you to notice the phrase *"the planting of the Lord."* In order to be the planting of the Lord, you must first dig a hole, however deep is necessary. Then you place the seed into the soil and cover the seed up.

As mentioned in Chapter 1, when that seed is in the soil, what does the soil provide for that seed? Well, the first thing it provides is warmth and nourishment. The soil provides what the seed needs: the minerals and moisture for the seed to be able to grow. The soil also provides resistance, which makes the seed strong.

The weight of the soil on the seed provides resistance to the budding plant so that when the plant breaks out of the kernel of the seed, it begins to move the weight of the soil. One of the reasons God designed it that way is so when the plant actually breaks through the soil and comes out into the sunlight, it is strong enough. When the wind blows hard and the sun beats down or the heavy rain pours, the plant can handle the elements that are actually going to bring the moisture, the warmth, and the light—everything that it needs to live. If the plant is not offered some resistance, the things intended to bring growth will actually bring death.

Growth Environment

The soil provides resistance, much like lifting weights provides resistance to our muscles to make them stronger. Healthy resistance creates an environment for us to grow and flourish. Most people live and die in a nongrowth environment. Some graduates from high school or college, have a tendency to stop developing themselves. Unless you learn to keep growing personally and developing yourself, you will stop growing.

As you continue to grow, you'll learn that it's important to work harder on yourself than you do on your job. If you work harder on yourself than you do on your job, you make more money at your job. Remember, money is attracted not pursued. Another way to say that—you bring value to the marketplace; you don't just bring time. This means you need to work on increasing your value.

One of the greatest things we can do for anyone who comes to work for us is to provide a growth environment where they can learn and grow. As a leader, we can help people gain knowledge, understanding, and wisdom. When employees are in that kind of environment, they can grow and become more than they are. If they do that, then you are empowering them to bring more to your organization.

I met up with H.B. London after I had spent time in the trenches of the Columbine shooting, officiating four of the funerals at our church. This late gentleman was considered a pastor to pastors and serves as Family Focus Vice President for many years. The second time we had lunch together, London told me about research his ministry had done. He said, "The average pastor has something happen twenty-three times a month that could be a significant hurt in his or her life." Someone says something or does something hurtful, or even rejects the pastor. If pastors have not learned how to handle that kind of emotional pain, they end up fostering a hurt. That's the reason why so many pastors leave the ministry never to return. Here's another statistic he gave me. He said, "It takes at least two years to get over a hurt." Well, if you get hurt twenty-three times a month, that starts to add up.

Sheep in the Midst of Wolves

In Matthew 10:16, Jesus says: *"Behold, I send you out as sheep in the midst of wolves. Therefore, be wise as serpents and harmless as doves."* The reason you're wise as a serpent and harmless as a dove is because you're going out in the midst of wolves.

It is wise to have perspective about other people—be wise as a serpent but harmless as a dove. When I hire people to work in my office, there are some things I can't afford to put up with. I can't afford to put up with certain levels of foolishness. We're dealing with money, and in most instances, it's other people's money. I can't afford employees to have a bad day when I'm doing certain things. They need to be on point.

John 2:23-25 (AMP) says:

Now when He was in Jerusalem at the Passover feast, many believed in His name [identifying themselves with Him] after seeing His signs (attesting miracles) which He was doing. But Jesus, for His part, did not entrust Himself to them, because He knew all people [and understood the superficiality and fickleness of human nature], and He did not need anyone to testify concerning man [and human nature], for He Himself knew what was in man [in their hearts—in the very core of their being].

Jesus had perspective without passing judgment. He understood. People ask me all the time how I work with volunteers. Well, the first thing is you can't entrust yourself to them. You cannot. You have to be wise as a serpent, harmless as a dove.

Four Kinds of People

When you lead, you're going to encounter four different types of people. The first are those who are spiritually unhealthy. The next are people who are spiritually immature. The third group you'll encounter are those who are spiritually mature, and the fourth are the spiritually giving. You can also substitute the word *spiritually* here for *emotionally*—emotionally unhealthy, emotionally immature, emotionally mature, and emotionally giving.

Why would I need to have perspective without passing judgment? It's not just because I know who to put on the team or who to put in a certain position. If I'm going to help them and lead them, I need to know how to direct them.

Let's say I meet you and I sense that you are spiritually mature. I'm not going to put you on the board after I've known you for one week. The first thing I'm going to do is invite you to the welcome class. I'm going to go through thirteen weeks of teaching. I want to get to know

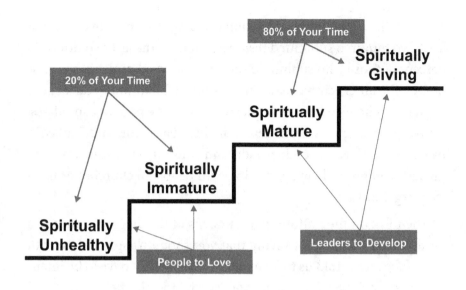

you so I can determine if you're going to be a leader. If you commit yourself for thirteen weeks, I know I've found a faithful person.

After the thirteen weeks, then 2 Timothy 2:2 comes into play: "...*Commit these to faithful men who will be able to teach others also.*" I'm not ready to commit everything to you yet. Now that you have graduated, I invite you to the leadership class. On top of that, I will ask you to help someone in a particular area. I'm not making you an official leader, yet. I want to observe how well you hold up in those roles.

I see your faithfulness in class. I see your faithfulness in leadership. I see your faithfulness in dealing with other people. Now I know that I have someone who is spiritually mature, and I can bring the person into our core dialogue schedule. I have a pipeline of leaders now who are coming through. I am screening and vetting them in a scriptural way so that I commit only to the faithful. You can "... *entrust to reliable people who will also be qualified to teach others*" (2 Timothy 2:2 NIV).

Every time I advertise a position on Craigslist in Denver, I get at least two hundred submitted resumes. Up until the last two times, 70 percent of those who submitted resumes for an administrative assistant or for an executive assistant position all had four-year college degrees. So here's what I do to narrow down the pool of candidates: I have people on my team research their Facebook and LinkedIn pages. They research each person and find out who they are. You must screen properly when dealing with people in churches or ministry organizations.

The folks on the bottom two stairsteps of the diagram can take a lot of your time. I'm not saying that you shouldn't spend time with these folks; Jesus told us to love everybody. You just have to be intentional and strategic about how you're going to help them.

Let's say I fly into Mexico City after an earthquake, and I'm a doctor. I have a group of nurses with me, and I start looking at the devastation. But let's say I spend all my time with the first person I find. What happens to all the other people who are dying and in dire need of medical care? They don't get any help. Therefore, I want to create a triage where I'm using my best skills to direct the people who work for me to help others as well.

As a leader, when we use the term "potential time wasters," it doesn't mean ignore those people entirely. It's about doing what God has called you to do in the best manner. I can either do this one individual at a time, or I can use the example of a triage and train people to help the others. So if the people in the bottom two stairs of the graph are taking up only 20 percent of my time, who is ministering to them? Those with whom I have spent 80 percent of my time equipping. The people who are spiritually mature or spiritually giving are the ones who are actually ministering to those who are spiritually immature or spiritually unhealthy.

We have to love these people, but we have to be wise as serpents and harmless as doves. When it comes to leading, your job is to raise up leaders. Your job is to raise up people who actually go and do the work of the ministry.

Ephesians 4:11-12 says that the role of the apostle, prophet, pastor, evangelist, and teacher is to edify the body, raise them up, and equip them. It means to equip as a soldier. You equip them so they can go out and fight the good fight of faith.

As mentioned previously, I love to fly-fish and sometimes I go to the South Platte River in Colorado. Some fly-fishermen there have $3,000 worth of equipment. I learned a long time ago that the equipment is not going to catch fish. They think that because they have several thousand dollars worth of equipment that they're going to be able to catch some fish. Likewise, while equipping potential leaders with materials is definitely important, I also have to take them out and actually show them *how* to fish. I spend the 80 percent of my time not just giving the leaders I'm raising up my material. Yes, I do that. But I'm also taking a deeper role in their life and really showing them how to do what I do.

Don't Take Ducks to Eagle School

A good leader doesn't put the bottom two stair-steppers on the team. It's better to put them in some kind of discipleship or recovery program to help them move up. The stairstep illustration shows how people can move, grow, and mature. I say it this way, "Don't take your ducks to eagle school." If you take your ducks to eagle school all they're going to do is quack, and all you're going to have is a bunch of quacking. You still have to love them, but you have to be strategic and intentional about how you help and where you place them.

That's why you have to create a system that you can recruit people into, not just recruit them to you. If you recruit people to you personally, it will give you an ego boost. But ultimately that's not good for them—and it's not good for you. Instead, recruit them to a system and put them in a growth environment, where the soil has the warmth, nourishment, and resistance to help them stand on their own. If you create a codependent environment, it means they will depend on you and not do anything on their own. They don't take the initiative to make a move. That really stunts your endeavor's success.

Order, Not Perfection

The key is to look for order, not perfection. You're never going to meet anybody who is perfect. So what can you do? First, you look for people who are available. Are they there when you need them? Do they have the ability to make appointments and be there?

Second, you look for people who are faithful. What does faithful mean? They show up on time. You can count on them to tackle projects with excellence. They're dependable. They take initiative to get things done. They keep their word and are consistent.

Finally, find people who are teachable. If people are teachable, that means they have humility to receive instruction or teaching. I'm looking for people who are available, faithful, and teachable. That's who I'm going to pour my life into.

- A: Available

- F: Faithful

- T: Teachable

The Pareto Principle

Early in my career, I pastored in the Bible Belt, but at the age of 30, I moved to Colorado. Jesse Duplantis came and preached for me at our Columbine church the first six months I was there.

After the first service, Jesse said to me, "Billy what are you doing here?"

"What do you mean?" I said.

"Man, you just left a great church in another state."

"God called me," I shrugged.

"Well, Billy, you've always dug it out of the ground. You're a dig-it-out-of-the-ground guy. But you know Colorado ain't the Bible Belt."

"Jesse, I've learned a bunch of stuff. I've only been here six months, but the first thing I learned is, 'Toto, you ain't in Kansas no more.'"

Colorado is *not* the Bible Belt.

Things weren't as easy. I realized that I was alone. I had just a few team members, so I didn't have a team who could help filter my schedule. On Sunday mornings, I'd always shake hands, make eye contact, and I had a conversation with people to get to know them. It helps build rapport. During that process, I developed an approach that helped me identify faithful people.

People would say to me, "Listen, my wife and I are going to go to lunch today at a nice steakhouse. We'd like to take you. Would you and your wife come with us to lunch?" During that season of time, I had about thirty people on Sunday morning who were coming to our church. That's everybody—kids, adults, everybody. So, when asked out for a meal, I would respond, "I really appreciate that invitation! But because we have young children, my wife and I don't go out to eat on Sundays. But if you'd like to have coffee on Tuesday or Thursday this week, I'd be delighted to meet you." I offered to be available. I just wasn't available on Sunday.

People on the first two stairsteps would get offended. I did it on purpose every time I was asked because I didn't have anyone else to manage my schedule.

Many people were offended that I wouldn't join them for lunch on Sunday. However, there were a few who wouldn't become offended, and that's who I had coffee with. Only 20 percent of people ever make it this far. This is who you spend 80 percent of your time with.

The Pareto Principle says that 20 percent of what you do gets 80 percent of the results. So, 80 percent of what you do only gets 20 percent of the result. When we're applying that principle to people, you want to spend 80 percent of your time with the 20 percent of faithful people—developing, coaching, and training them. Use available, faithful, teachable people to develop leaders.

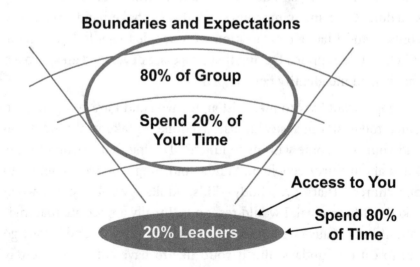

Boundaries and Expectations

80% of Group

Spend 20% of
Your Time

Access to You

20% Leaders

Spend 80%
of Time

Second, give them expectations. The following is a leadership funnel showing how faithful people will rise to meet expectations and become leaders themselves.

An example of expectations would be what I mentioned earlier about inviting people to a welcome class. If they faithfully attended the class, then I would invite them to a leadership class. If they faithfully participated in *that,* then I would place them in a small role or task.

If they were faithful with that too, then I would offer them more and more responsibility until they themselves turn around to develop other leaders.

Remember, we look for order, not perfection. Look for order in these five areas:

1. Faith

2. Feelings

3. Finances

4. Friends

5. Family

When it comes to their *faith,* a good question to consider is what is their daily walk with the Lord? Do they have a daily prayer life? Are they reading the Bible consistently?

When it comes to their *feelings,* are they emotionally consistent? Or do they often have up-and-down days? How do they get along with others?

When it comes to their *finances,* are they overly distracted? Do they always need financial help? Or on the opposite end of the spectrum, are they so focused on making money that they have no time for God?

When it comes to their *friends,* do they keep good company? Are their friends leading them *toward* the things of God or *away* from the things of God?

When it comes to *family,* is the husband and wife's relationship one of love and harmony, or are they disagreeing constantly? Do their children seem to be happy and well-behaved?

Please do not misunderstand my intention here in this teaching—we are not looking for perfect people. No one is perfect but Jesus. And while we should not pass judgment upon people, we do need to gain perspective on them and care for them accordingly.

CHAPTER 7

THE LEADER AND CRITICISM

Have you ever heard the saying, "When you're the one on the ladder, all others see is your backside?" Many times, those who are following see the leader from that perspective. Those you are leading many times do not have the same perspective on things because they are seeing things from a different position. In the early 1990s, John Maxwell, author and leadership expert, helped me through his teachings to better understand how to deal with criticism as a leader. Much of what I write in this chapter came from what I learned from him and from my own experience.

Over the years, I have been criticized for things that I deserved to be criticized for—and I have been criticized for things that I didn't deserved to be criticized for. None of us are perfect, so we will make mistakes and we will be criticized for them. Remember, Moses was criticized by his own family.

*One day Miriam and Aaron were **criticizing** Moses because his wife was a Cushite woman, and they said, "Has the Lord spoken only through Moses? Hasn't he spoken through us, too?" But the Lord heard them. Immediately* *he summoned Moses, Aaron, and Miriam to the Tabernacle: "Come here, you three," he commanded. So they stood before the Lord. (Now Moses was the humblest man on earth.) Then the Lord descended in the Cloud and stood at the entrance of the Tabernacle. "Aaron and Miriam, step forward," he commanded; and they did. And the Lord said to them, "Even with a prophet, I would communicate by visions and dreams; but that is not how I communicate with my servant Moses. He is completely at home in my house! With him I speak face-to-face! And he shall see the very form of God! Why then were you not afraid to **criticize** him?" Then the anger of the Lord grew hot against them, and he departed. As the Cloud moved from above the Tabernacle, Miriam suddenly became white with leprosy. When Aaron saw what had happened, he cried out to Moses, "Oh, sir, do not punish us for this sin; we were fools to do such a thing. Don't let her be as one dead, whose body is half rotted away at birth." And Moses cried out to the Lord, "Heal her, O God, I beg you!" And the Lord said to Moses, "If her father had but spit in her face she would be defiled seven days. Let her be banished from the camp for seven days, and after that she can come back again." So Miriam was excluded from the camp for seven days, and the people waited until she was brought back in before they traveled again* (Numbers 12:1-15 The Living Bible).

It could be up for debate on whether or not Moses missed it by marrying a Cushite woman. I think that he did. So, Miriam and Aaron might have been in their rights as family to question the marriage, but they took their criticism a step too far by asking, *"Has the Lord spoken only through Moses?"* In other words, they began to question whether or not Moses was the leader whom God had anointed to lead the children of Israel. God let them know that they were wrong for questioning Moses' authority to lead.

If you are called by God to lead, whether it is in ministry or business or both, you have been set in authority by God over that enterprise. You will make mistakes because you are still human. However, just because you make a mistake in leading others does not mean you are to abdicate your place of leadership and authority. Parents can make mistakes with their children but it doesn't mean that they stop being parents.

The temptation for some people is to criticize you when you make a mistake and take it further by questioning your authority and leadership at all levels. God let Moses' family know that was not right.

Putting Criticism in Proper Perspective

The statements and questions that follow will help you put the criticism that you may receive in proper perspective.

1. Determine if the purpose was to build up or tear down.

If someone is criticizing you, ask yourself, *Is this to hurt me or to help me?* Many times criticism is from people projecting their hurts or anger onto you as a leader. I call this "emotional dumping." It's important to know the difference between criticism that is "self-projecting" and criticism intended to help you see where you may have a blind spot.

2. Ascertain the person's attitude. Was it judgmental or gentle?

3. Consider if the criticism occurred in public or private.

I can guarantee you that any legitimate criticism will always be told to you in private. If someone is judging you before your home group or specialty group, and the criticism is constantly coming in a public setting, that is a pretty good sign that the criticism is meant to hurt you.

If you are the one criticizing, why does the criticism need to be private and not public? First of all, you're not trying to lead a rebellion. If you're truly trying to help the leader, you won't degrade his or her authority. It's nobody else's business what you have to say to the leader. Even if it is other people's business, they don't need to know it in that setting.

4. Analyze if the criticism was said out of personal hurt or for personal benefit.

Many times criticism comes out of someone's personal hurt. It's important that you make the differentiation. Most criticism comes off as legitimate, but the real issue is what's in their own heart.

When I first started pastoring, I was 24 years old. I didn't know a lot. I still don't know a lot, but I certainly knew less then than I do now. There was a very well-known businessman in the local community and we had a friendly relationship for three or four months or so. We talked, had coffee together, and all of those things. All of a sudden, he began to criticize me about the finances of the church. At that time I wasn't even handling the finances. I didn't even see what came in and went out. We were an Assembly of God church with a secretary/treasurer and the whole nine yards. We voted on when the toilet paper was supposed to be bought—we did all of that. I couldn't figure out why he was criticizing me about the finances, which was an aspect of the church where I had no involvement. As a matter of fact, at that particular time, I was getting paid a minimum amount of money.

The more I visited with this man, the more he criticized. Come to find out, he had filed bankruptcy five times. Usually, people will criticize you in areas that they have a hard time with.

5. Identify the source of the criticism.

You always need to know the person who's criticizing. If somebody comes and says, "This was said about such and such in the church," my first question always is, "Who said it?" Why is that my first question? If the person has a pattern of criticism in his or her own life, it's probably a pretty good sign that it's not about you.

Identify the source and you will know how legitimate the criticism is. In other words, you have to be able to size up the situation and consider the source. Most of us let whiners keep us from being winners. It's amazing how a good strong leader, if he or she is not careful, will give into the dictates of a whiner and change the whole flow of the ministry because a person doesn't like it. Think what Jesus would have done!

Let me give you the other side of this. If the criticism comes from people who normally don't criticize and generally have a positive attitude, I listen intently. They're probably seeing something I don't see.

6. Compare people's problems with their criticisms.

People have a tendency to project their own problems onto other people. As a leader that's a big issue. Jesus says in Matthew 22:39 that we need to love our neighbor as ourselves. The key here is if people don't love themselves, they sure won't love you. If people are angry at themselves, you can bank on it, they're going to be angry at you. They'll make it seem like you're the problem as the leader! Quit owning other people's problems. There's a real key there as you learn to grow and handle the situation as it needs to be handled. Compare people's problems to their criticisms.

7. Realize that even good leaders get criticized.

John chapter 6 is actually a teaching on leadership. It teaches you how to deal with other people.

> From this time many of his disciples turned back and no longer followed him. "You do not want to leave too, do you?" Jesus asked the Twelve. Simon Peter answered him, "Lord, to whom shall we go? You have the words of eternal life. We have come to believe and to know that you are the Holy One of God (John 6:66-69 NIV).

I want you to realize that even good leaders get criticized and followers leave them. This Scripture passage in John 6 tells us that followers even left Jesus. They left His church, they left His home group, they left His district—they left the greatest Teacher who ever lived!

Young pastors call me and ask if there is any advice I could give them as they start their church. I don't ask them how much of the Bible they know. I don't ask how brilliant they are in their theological dissertations. I don't care about that. I want to know how they handle people. Why? Because the first time somebody leaves, if they don't understand what's going on, they will be devastated. Most pastors quit the ministry because of that one reason. Most leadership in the church quit because of relationships with other people.

Sometimes there's not a whole lot you can do to keep somebody from going or leaving. Jesus couldn't and you can't. What you want to do is you want to blame yourself, then you want to get angry and blame them. Let's forget about blaming them or blaming yourself and just realize it's going to happen. It's the normal way life works. People leave. Don't blame them, don't criticize them, but don't blame yourself either. Just realize it's the principle of life.

8. Dispel the myth—their problem is because of you.

Do you remember the initials E.G.R? It means *Extra Grace Required*. EGRs and your own guilt will make you think you could have done more.

I remember a particular situation where a lady led the praise and worship, and she did a good job. The problem was every Sunday morning she would go on and on and on speaking in tongues over the microphone. When I say on and on, I don't mean a message and interpretation and everybody shouted and hen went on to to the next song. I mean she would take fifteen minutes to speak in tongues. The pastor asked her to stop because the church had a lot of people who didn't understand it. He told her that if she was going to do it—give a message, get an interpretation, and move on decently and in order. This woman was offended.

When I spoke to the pastor about it, I asked him about the lady's marriage. He said, in essence, she "wore the pants." Next, I asked about her father. The pastor said that just the other day the lady was talking about how she hadn't forgiven her father for things he had done to her. Then I knew the root of the problem—she didn't respect any kind of authority. She'd been hurt, she was upset, and the last thing she needed was to be behind a microphone in front of everybody, unless she was walking through recovery.

Her problem was not the leader's fault even though she was blaming him for it.

When someone comes into the life of your business or your organization, you need to locate where the person is spiritually and relationally. With the help of the Holy Spirit, understand where that person is on his or her spiritual growth scale. The people who criticize you the most are people who are going through recovery.

If you're so sensitive that anytime somebody says something the least bit negative, you put up your fists and say let's fight, you've got a problem, right? You have to be able to love and accept people, size them up, and then you will know how to deal with them. Why? Because your whole goal as a leader is to help them get better at serving God.

9. Ask what they like.

Turn the conversation from the negative to the positive. If you find out what people like about your ministry, it may give more credibility to what they're saying because that means they really have thought through it. They're not just dumping emotionally or projecting their hurt into the situation.

When you ask what they like, it may help to direct you to meeting their individual or family needs. As leaders, we're really meant to help people.

A prominent man (Frank Sotomayor) visited my church while I was pastoring, and he said something to me one weekend that caught me off guard. He said, "You know one of the things that attracted me to this church? One Sunday you were standing outside shaking hands and I was coming by. One of the first things you said to me was, "Listen, if you need us to help you find a church, we'll be glad to help you." Then you listed some of the churches and I was impressed. I thought, *This guy is recommending me to go somewhere else. I'm coming to church here!* The point is that, yes, I want everybody to attend my church, but the real point is that we want people to find the best place where they fit; that may not be your church or your business.

10. Determine how broad the criticism is.

Now why is this important? It determines the validity of the criticism. If it is broad-based, you better listen. This will help pinpoint if the problem really is with everybody and everything, or if there is something more specific the person is worried about.

A man came to me in the first church I pastored; he was on our church board. He told me everyone felt this negative way about something. It was a family church, so I figured he was probably right. I called another member of the board devastated. He started laughing at me on the phone! I thank God I had some mature men around me who could knock some sense into me.

He said, "Well, Brother Epperhart, here's what I'd like you to do. I'd like you to go back into that board meeting and ask this question. First I want you to read off what the problem is and give the response so-and-so gave to you. Then ask, 'Now does everybody feel this way?'"

So I did that. I went into the board meeting with my little yellow pad where I had it written down. My heart was pitter pattering and I was sweating and shaking. Here I am all of 23 years of age and I'm sweating thinking about this conversation. I read the statement and asked if everybody felt that way. The sister of the guy who told me everybody felt that way, immediately spoke up and said, "I don't feel that way." Then his mother spoke up and said to her son, "How could you say such a thing?" True story—I'll never forget it as long as I live.

When somebody says, "Everybody feels a certain way" the first thing I do is ask, "Who specifically feels that way? Give me their names." I can tell you without reservation that in seventeen years of fulltime pastoral ministry, it has never been true that "everybody feels this way."

It's important that you don't buy into the line. It also is important that you determine how broad-based the criticism is in order to determine the validity. When somebody uses broad-based criticism, it's usually because they're trying to champion their own agenda.

11. Maintain a right attitude.

The last thing you want to do is get defensive. I have learned in the past that it's pretty good to have a little righteous indignation at certain times, but you need to keep your attitude right. If you get hurt and defensive, there is no way you can deal with the issue in any objective way.

So if you feel defensive, what should you do? You need other people around you to give you some perspective. Fellow leaders can tell you how they dealt with a similar issue. I can tell you as a leader, the number one thing you need to be responsible for personally is you absolutely must keep your attitude right. It's okay to get with some healthy people who are in leadership with you, or above you in leadership, to vent how you feel. It is not okay to continue to vent that. It's okay to say, "I'm hurt! I don't understand! Give me some perspective!" It is not okay to camp out there.

12. Offer resistance.

What's important here is that you and I as leaders should always be accepting of people regardless of where they are initially. Now what I mean by that is, let's learn to accept people at face value. If somebody says he or she has a problem, we accept the fact there is a problem. If somebody is challenged by something, accept the fact that there is a challenge. But as they continue to come to you with criticism, or as they continue to come to you with that same problem, you need to begin to offer resistance.

Learn to set boundaries, because if you don't, you're facilitating their negative behavior. You could easily become codependent in a relationship like that. If they keep criticizing, you need to make sure you determine what the real problem is.

In leadership, you need to ask questions! It may be the first time some people have been offered healthy resistance. Therefore, because of that, they may be able to grow and learn. The real key to leadership is to care enough for your people that you don't care what they think about you, as long as you put them first and you're trying to help them. Most of us do not offer resistance, because we're afraid of what the other person will think about us. The problem with that is that we're really not loving them if we're not willing to help them through what they're facing.

I want to warn you, though, the only reason you should be offering resistance is for the good of that person and or for the good of the group. You're not offering resistance for your good. If you're doing it for your good—that's the wrong motivation. If you're doing it to protect yourself, that's the wrong motivation.

Always ask "what" questions, not "why" questions. Why leads to their subjective insight, what leads to a specific issue. You're asking for their opinion when you ask why. When you're asking what, you're asking for the issue.

If my child comes home from school and says there's a problem with a teacher, my first question is always what. I don't want to keep it on the level of their emotional hurt. I want to get to the level of the issue. Do I need to take time to deal with the emotional hurt? Absolutely. But I want to deal with emotional hurt *after* I've dealt with the issue. If not, the conversation devolves into a black hole of emotional hurt the child and I will struggle to climb out of.

13. Diagnose fatigue.

When you're fatigued, everything is magnified. You're too tired to deal with anything. Your emotions usually are wiped out. That tiredness sometimes causes you to want to run. When you're fatigued, there's no real spiritual or emotional resources to deal with things. Even the smallest anthill begins to look like a mountain because emotionally or spiritually you don't have the strength to even go over the ant hill.

Usually if you're fatigued you're dealing with everything at a felt-need level rather than a real-need level. If something comes up and you have a short fuse, you will obviously overreact. You're going to deal with it just out of frustration. When your body is tired and you're in a negative mode, it doesn't matter what comes up, you're going to be negative.

Sometimes people you are leading or dealing with are fatigued as well. Not only do you react on a short fuse whenever you're fatigued, whenever they're fatigued they react on a short fuse. As a leader, you have to understand at what fatigue level your people are to help you understand why they're reacting like they are.

14. Surround yourself with positive people.

Something happened to me this week that we'll discuss in our board of advisors meeting. It was fairly negative having to do with the building and the tenants. About an hour after the situation, my friend Al Jandl called. He talked to my wife, and then I called him back. He talked to me for a long time. Afterward, I felt a whole lot better. I had talked to a person who was removed from the location and able to see things objectively. He spoke positives into our lives.

The greatest lesson I ever learned about criticism was from other people who were in leadership. If you do anything right in your life, you're going to be criticized. It doesn't matter what you do or don't do—you're going to get criticized. Hey, guess what, your adult kids one day are going to criticize you. You know those little precious four- and five-year-olds right now? One day after they're grown up, they will tell you that you don't know anything. One of the best kinds of positive people are the people who've been where you are and can share good news with you. That's the best kind of people to be around.

15. Don't lose sight of your calling.

Listen to me. Don't let criticism steal your calling in life. The Southern Baptist denomination issued about three years ago a statistic about their pastors. Over 50 percent of their pastors were quitting the ministry permanently. Over 50 percent! My encouragement to you as a leader is not to lose sight of your calling because somebody criticizes you. Sometimes we do that enough ourselves. When you start listening to other people rather than God and His will for your life, you'll definitely lose sight of your unique calling or destiny.

CHAPTER 8

THE LEADER AND FAMILY

Five Characteristics of a Healthy Family

F amilies come in all sizes and forms, whether a single adult with no children, a couple with several children, a single parent, a blended family, or any other family type. No matter the format, these five characteristics apply to all family types. And it's up to the leader of the family to implement them.

In Genesis 2:18-24 (AMP), we read:

Now the Lord God said, "It is not good (beneficial) for the man to be alone; I will make him a helper [one who balances him—a counterpart who is] suitable and complementary for him." So the Lord God formed out of the ground every animal of the field and every bird of the air, and brought them to Adam to see what he would call them; and whatever the man called a living creature, that was its name. And the man gave names to all the livestock, and to the birds of the air, and to every animal of the field; but for Adam there was not found a helper [that was] suitable (a companion) for him. So the Lord God caused a deep sleep to fall upon Adam; and while he slept, He took one of his ribs and closed up the flesh at that place. And the rib which the Lord God had taken from the man He made (fashioned, formed) into a woman, and He brought her and presented her to the man. Then Adam said, "This is now bone of my bones, and flesh of my flesh; she shall be called Woman, because she was taken out of Man." For this reason a man shall leave his father and his mother, and shall be joined to his wife; and they shall become one flesh.

We know from the Word of God that *family* is the first institution God gave to humankind. This means that it is important for us to understand how the family should work. In other words, how did God intend for us as a family to communicate and to connect? My studies of Scripture have lead me to five characteristics that describe a healthy family.

A lot of this comes from my personal experience in raising a family—our two children and four grandchildren.

For I have known (chosen, acknowledged) him [as My own], so that he may teach and command his children and [the sons of] his household after him to keep the way of the Lord by doing what is righteous and just, so that the Lord may bring upon Abraham what He has promised him (Genesis 18:19 AMP).

#1: Unconditional Love and Communication

The first characteristic of a healthy family is showing unconditional love. First John 4:10 (AMP) says, *"In this is love, not that we loved God, but that He loved us and sent His son to be the propitiation [or sacrifice]...for our sins."* Romans 5:8 says, *"But God demonstrates*

His own love toward us, in that while we were still sinners, Christ died for us." This first characteristic is also the most important.

Let's establish something quickly—unconditional love does not primarily come through the words we speak. Sometimes, we think we are off the hook just because we *said*, "I love you." But the truth of the matter is that the words we speak are only 7 percent of the total communication package. Your tone of voice makes up another 38 percent of communication, while your body language constitutes a whopping *55 percent!*

This means we cannot just hide behind our words or text messages. For starters, though, if you don't actively tell your children or your spouse that you love them, start verbalizing those three words now and *often*. But I'm under the assumption that a lot of us may be able to physically say, "I love you"—so let's go to the next level. Let's tackle that other 93 percent of communication.

If you want to communicate love to your wife, chances are you are not going to take her out to McDonald's for a Big Mac and fries. No, you step up the game! You put out rose petals, but they don't lead to the bedroom; they lead to the dinner table. That communicates a deeper level of interest in your wife as a person. It communicates that you love her in a deeper way.

In the same vein, you shouldn't rush to the store the morning of her birthday and spend two minutes picking out a decent toaster. Instead, go to the mall and spend time buying all the stuff that you might not like or think about as a man. If you don't like it, that might be a good indication that you should buy it. And if you get embarrassed to be in the mall, put on a cap, a false mustache, and some sunglasses so no one will recognize you!

When I was much younger, I once went shopping for my wife at the mall and picked a place to shop because it was really pink.

A young lady greeted me with a standard, "Can I help you?"

"Yes, what do you have for my wife?" I said. "I'm in a hurry! Can you please help me?"

"Well, a lot of women like lotions and bubble baths," she offered.

"Great, I'll take them all."

"You're kidding!"

"I'll take them all! How many do you have?"

"Well, there's a lot!" she said.

"I'll take them all! How fast can you get them in a sack?"

You would have thought she was shopping for herself. She picked up one of everything. Meanwhile, I was trying to leave discreetly so no one would see me. She filled three massive pink bags and puts pink tissue on top of each one. I left loaded down my weight in pink packaging! All I could think was, *My God, what if somebody from church sees me.*

I booked it for the exit when suddenly, "Pastor, pastor hold up!" I tried to act like I didn't hear him, but he finally caught me red-handed. At least I had made it to the Sears tool section by that point!

Despite that momentary embarrassment, it was worth it to me to communicate my love boldly and loudly to my wife. Of course, now you can just order online—but do your research and order ahead of time! No one wants to open up a gift only to find a picture and a promise that it will arrive in the mail soon.

During my pastoring days, I did some home visits in a Louisiana town. There was one house in particular that struck me. During the visit, a little girl kept coming in and reaching up to her mother. Finally, after several attempts, her mother pushed her away.

This little girl was *not* annoying. I have been in homes where a big Great Dane jumped on me and pinned me to the couch! It started licking my face, and I thought, *Someone please get this dog off me!* I have also been in homes where the children do keep interrupting—loudly! This little girl wasn't really interrupting, though. She was just quietly reaching out toward her mother. My curiosity finally bested me and I asked the mother why she didn't hug her daughter. She told me that they don't hug in their house.

That broke my heart. In a healthy home, unconditional love is communicated through body language—and that includes physical affection.

We've all had those rough days when we get home and a spouse or parent asks, "How was your day?" *Fine.* "Who did you talk to?" *Nobody.* "What did you do today?" *Nothing.* Your family is trying to communicate with you, but you are shutting them down.

Communication and unconditional love mean showering our spouses with love and opening up to them even when we don't feel like doing so. It means entering their world and doing the things they want to do.

When we were newlyweds, my wife would always tell me, "Honey, if you want to spend time with me, don't take me camping." See, my idea of spending quality time was taking a 9-foot camper out and staying for a week on the lake. I would fish and she could cook the fish.

Now, some women enjoy that kind of thing! But Becky's idea of quality time is more in the realm of taking a trip to New York, staying in the Plaza Hotel, eating roast goose over apple strudel at the Waldorf-Astoria, taking carriage rides around Central Park, and maybe squeezing in a Broadway show or two!

Unconditional love to me means learning about my family. What do they like to do? How can I be a blessing to them as a father, husband, and leader?

Of course, the same rule applies to wives. Show your husband unconditional love by doing the things that interest him sometimes.

When you show unconditional love, make sure it is in physical and emotional ways that fully communicate the truth of it.

I believe that one of America's greatest challenges right now is that people do not know how to develop healthy emotional bonds with one another. There's a reason we have a high divorce rate and absent fathers. To fight this, we need to build and maintain an emotional bond with each other. We need to be in tune with our family. That can never happen unless you're willing to invest in them. You can invest in your family by spending time doing the things they want to do. You can invest in them by blessing them through chores. You can, and should, invest in them by communicating openly and with affection. If you do not do these things, there will never be an emotional bond.

Men cannot act like cavemen coming up from the man cave and grunting when it comes to communication with our spouses and children. I challenge even the single men reading this to develop your emotional life so that you can communicate and build emotional bonds.

Love your family when the rest of the world won't. Make sure you look your children in the eyes and tell them that you are their fix-it-up person. Tell them that no matter what breaks, you'll work on fixing it. And if it can't be fixed, let them know you'll never give up trying. In other words, let them know you care, and you're there for them.

Give them an avenue to succeed. Unconditional love is displayed in the Bible. *"In this is love, not that we loved God, but that He loved us and sent His Son to be the propitiation for our sins"* (1 John 4:10).

In other words, as parents, it's not that our kids love us, it's that we love them, care for them, and show them that. That's the same for spouses. One person said, "If you want heat out of a stove, you've got to put some wood in first." It works the same way with love. We've got to be able to sow love and give love even when we feel like we're not getting anything in return.

#2: Family Traditions

Family traditions bring order and stability in your family. These traditions can include vacations, holidays, birthdays—even going out to eat. It's any time you can create a consistent expectation that something is going to happen. You are going to show up as a family and do something together. Think about Christmas.

One year, Becky and I asked our young-adult children, "What are some of the things you really remember about Christmas from your childhood?" One of the things they both brought up was how we would always make tea cakes together. Tea cakes are a type of dessert, and the tradition came from my wife's 96-year-old grandmother. She was born in 1892, and every Christmas she made two things: homespun and tea cakes. We picked up the tea cake tradition. Traditions like this bring warmth and fond memories to your children and your whole family.

Another family tradition was to take an annual vacation. We did everything from going to the lake to waterskiing to taking more exotic European vacations. We went as a family to New York several times. This annual rhythm established tradition and fun.

One time a father asked me, "What do you do when you have a fourteen-year-old son who doesn't want to spend any time with you?" I told him, "You find out what he likes to do and you go do that with him." So he went out and bought his son one of the best skateboards money could buy. Now it's not about things, but by doing that, he was showing his son how important he was as a son to him. The father started taking his son to different, cool places to go skateboarding. Today, because of that, this man and his adult children have a great relationship.

Maybe you're reading this book and there are traditions you haven't yet established. Start today doing things that establish family time together that can then become a family tradition, whether sitting around the table playing games or going on a yearly vacation. Make sure it's something that every member in the family enjoys doing.

Children don't know how to communicate this, but they really want to know they have parents they can depend on. A five-year-old isn't going to wake up and use the word *depend*. But in their hearts, they need dependability and stability from their parents to become a healthy and happy individual. Family traditions help establish that.

#3: Commitment of Time

When my son was much younger, I wanted to spend some quality time with him. I decided to take him fishing, one of my favorite activities. We went to a lake up in the mountains on the boat I owned at that time. I found out that my son didn't really enjoy fishing. After some prodding, I realized it was simply because he didn't know how to do it. Here I am, all excited about *my* favorite activity, but he doesn't even know what to do. I had to slow down and take time to walk him through it. Was it particularly exciting for me to put my own fun aside and teach him? Not really. Was it fun for me to simply be with him and teach him my favorite sport? Yes!

It's important to find things your family members enjoy doing. Enter their world a little bit. Several years ago, I hated to golf. After a while, I got tired of chasing the ball. But Brant, my son, really enjoys it and so we play to spend quality time. I get to enter his world; once I'm there, I find I enjoy doing things he enjoys *with* him.

You've got to make the commitment of time. It's not just about what you like to do. When we understand these things, we can really build the kind of family God wants us to have.

A healthy family makes the commitment of time to one another. Statistics from the University of Michigan Institute of Social Research say that working mothers spend eleven minutes of quality time each weekday with their children and thirty minutes a day on the weekends. It's amazing that we don't realize how little time we spend with our children.

That same research revealed that fathers spend eight minutes of quality time on the weekdays and only eleven minutes on the weekend with their children. One of the things that stood out to me when I was a minister during the Columbine tragedy was something Josh McDowell, author of *Evidence That Demands a Verdict,* said to me. He said, "Billy, what's amazing is that we are beginning to live today in a fatherless society." Then he said something that I had never researched myself. He told me that over 75 percent of the males in prison never had a father figure in their lives.

The point is, there are challenges to actually spending the kind of time we need to spend with our children. But a healthy family makes the commitment to each other. So here are a couple of areas of time where you should be available.

Make time for your marriage. This is really important if you have children. The children will watch how you relate to one another. I've said for years that the home is a laboratory for human relationships. If you want to see your children become healthy adults, learn how as a husband and wife to relate to one another, care for one another, and communicate—eye contact, physical touch, body language, etc. That behavior is modeled for your children. What they see modeled before them is what they become. If they see their father loving and cherishing his wife, they'll do the same. If they see the wife respecting and reverencing her husband, they will model that as well.

Make time for each child. You should not only spend time together as a family but as individuals. In fact, one of the things that has been tremendously challenging in this day and age is for a family to sit down at a table and eat a meal together. Too many families are on their cellphones reading and texting or the television is on. We need to turn off all these distractions and communicate face-to-face as a family. Make sure that you actually have time to take each child on a personal date, whether you're the father or the mother.

Make all-together family time. This is where real bonding can happen as well. For example, during the Christmas season many families get together and reunite with people they haven't seen for several months or even a few years. It's amazing when you all get together, you can get right back into the love and fun if you came from a healthy family.

There should be unscheduled time. This is time that just serendipitously happens. Unscheduled times can be the very best times you spend together. Just the other day I went to see one of my grandson's play basketball. I thought they were playing a game that day, but they were actually just practicing. So I watched him practice for a while, but my two older grandsons said, "Poppa, let's go play." There was a football field nearby, and it was a beautiful, sunny day in Colorado. We spent an hour playing football together. I can't tell you how big of a deal that was for me—and them.

Make planned, fun times. One of my mentors told me that he took his children somewhere fun every Saturday night. They did this right up until the kids left home. What was unusual to me about that story was that the dad was a minister. He had to be up early every Sunday morning. Yet on Saturday night, he took his family out for fun times together! He said it was one of the most beneficial activities he did.

Another mentor told me, "Don't forget to have fun with your family and don't let the kids feel the pressure of the family." Sometimes in emotionally unhealthy homes, everything negative going on in the house is talked about, and the kids feel the pressure of that. I'm not saying don't be authentic, I'm just saying protect them.

The term *husband* literally comes from the words *house band*. It's the band that goes around the barrel that protects and keeps the barrel together. The word *wife* comes from the word *weaver*. So the wife weaves the details of the home together with the children, and the husband provides the actual protection. When you function as a husband and a wife and do that properly, fun times can be had and everyone can be healthy.

#4: Every Family Member Is Valued

Ephesians 2:10 says, "For we are His workmanship, created in Christ Jesus for good works, which God prepared beforehand that we should walk in them." In other words, we have value before God because we are God's workmanship.

You need to affirm the value of each of your family members so that they can be secure in the value placed in them by God. When they feel valued, they will value others. When every member of the family affirms the value of every other member, it creates a beautiful dance. This is one of the best foundations for building a healthy family.

Sometimes we get so busy that we don't really take the time to connect and bond. I like to say it this way: A healthy family has healthy bonds and healthy boundaries.

One of the best things that a father and a mother can do with their children is learn how to emotionally bond with their children.

It's important to keep this bonding process active as they get older. I can tell you that as they enter those teenager years, there can be an emotional separation. That's when you really have to turn up the emotional bonding activities with your children to keep them connected to you.

How we treat one another in the family is really how we're going to treat other people. That's again where the home becomes a laboratory for relationships in society. In fact, if a person is from a healthy family with good relationships, it's more than likely that the person has healthy relationships as an adult. That person's value has been affirmed by the family. So instead of walking into society insecure and disconnected, they're walking in secure and healthy and happy. That helps them relate to and be a blessing to other people. We really learn how to treat people by how we treat our family members.

The silent expressions you have in the family communicate much more than what you actually say with your mouth. A certain look in the eyes can convey criticism. Body language can convey anger. So sometimes it's the silent expressions that say more than what we actually say. Here's a poem, *Children Learn What They Live* written by Dorothy Law Nolte, that I really love:

> *If children live with criticism, they learn to condemn.*
> *If children live with hostility, they learn to fight.*
> *If children live with ridicule, they learn to be shy.*
> *If children live with shame, they learn to feel guilty.*
> *If children live with encouragement, they learn confidence.*
> *If children live with tolerance, they learn to be patient.*
> *If children live with praise, they learn to appreciate.*
> *If children live with acceptance, they learn to love.*

If children live with approval, they learn to like themselves.
If children live with honesty, they learn truthfulness.
If children live with security,
they learn to have faith in themselves and others.
If children live with friendliness,
they learn the world is a nice place in which to live.

In other words, the environment of a family really creates who is coming out of that family. That's why we need to have a healthy family. Here are a couple of steps for ensuring that is the outcome of your family.

A healthy family should affirm every individual's value—husband, wife, and each child. But let's talk about affirming the child's value. The following are a few healthy ways to build your child's self-worth:

Let them know that they belong in your family so that they are secure. More likely than not, if you give the child a feeling that they belong and are accepted, it increases their self-worth. When they are older and confronted with the kinds of destructive behaviors that many people get tempted with, they will have a strong enough sense of self-worth to not participate. Let them know your home is their home and they're always welcome.

In fact, I may shock you with this statement, but I'm going to write it anyway. It's more important for you to be a healthy family than a religious family. Of course, I believe that your relationship with God is vitally important. But sometimes people become full of fear and almost antagonistic in their fear—and they do it in the guise of religion.

I believe we must always learn to be positive in our faith. We can be aware of the dangers around us without being full of fear. Sometimes there are things in religion, not in Christ, that are unhealthy for people if they're not careful about how they deal with it. Anytime something takes away from the self-worth of a child and has to do with religion, it's not good. The Bible doesn't do that; Jesus doesn't do that.

Give your children a feeling that they are worthwhile. Find things to praise them about. A while back, *The One-Minute Manager* book was published. It talked about one-minute praisings and one-minute reprimands. That means that when you discipline a child or correct them, it should be short, quick, effective—and done with when it's over. Do the same with praising. Always be active with your praise in building up your child, as well as your reprimands when they're necessary. Be active, but don't camp out there. Do it, deal with it, talk about it, and move on. You want to create a feeling that they're worthwhile and you can do that by giving them praise about what they've accomplished.

Give them a feeling of confidence. I like to tell this story I heard several years ago. A little boy and his dad went to play baseball. The boy took a baseball and a bat and swung the bat as hard as he could and his dad yelled, "Strike one!" A second time he swung as hard as he could. His dad yelled, "Strike two!" The third time, he swung again, and his dad yelled, "Strike three!" The little boy looked at his dad and said, "See, Dad, I told you I'm a good pitcher." So when we talk about giving our kids a feeling of confidence, well that kid already had a lot of confidence. It's important even in their failures that they understand to have confidence.

#5: An Emotionally Safe Home

Another important factor of a healthy home is that it is an emotionally stable environment. The home is a laboratory for how we are to communicate with other people in society. How we treat each other at home will leak into every situation outside the home. It's a known fact that many violent teenagers come from violent homes. So much of this anger and violence could be prevented if adult men and women worked to be emotionally consistent in their lives, especially at home.

In alcoholic homes, a child might come home from school and have no idea what condition their father or mother will be in due to their drinking problem. They might not even expect their parent to be home to take care of them. Will their mom be sober tonight? Will she be up or down? Happy or sad? Will their dad be drunk and violent? They won't know what emotions to expect from their parent day in and day out. We *need* parents in homes who are emotionally consistent. We need parents who aren't lashing out at everyone around them just because they had a bad day. Children should be able to come home and feel safe and secure because they know their parents are emotionally consistent.

This doesn't mean we have to become robots or wear masks! It just means that we need to learn healthy mechanisms for distilling our stress so that we don't dump it on our families. It's time for all men and women, spouses and parents to learn how to grow up emotionally. It's time to overcome our past and our odds. It doesn't matter in the grand scheme of things what your dad was like or what your ex-husband did—your children will suffer if you don't rise to the challenge. I'm challenging you for the sake of your family.

When I was young, my family lived across the street from a lady who had been in the church for a long time. I called her Sister Stump. She was like another mom to me. Anytime I walked into her house, she would be somewhere singing and praising God.

I practically spent my first eighteen years of life in that house! I was with them all the time; I even vacationed with them. I got to see those parents in the good times, bad times, hard times, even the evil times. I know what they were like and I can say with absolute certainty that I never once heard her get angry or raise her voice. Sister Stump was the real deal. When she was praising God, she was truly praising God.

Of course, she is the exception. I would have to be disqualified if raising your voice was a disqualifier! But I will say that with her I never saw it. I would see her washing dishes while singing "Hallelujah, praise the Lord!" The neighbor boy and I would get in mud up to our ears and make a neighbor mad. All she would say was, "Now boys, you know you're not supposed to do that! Get in here and get yourselves cleaned off." We'd go into her house to get cleaned up, and she'd say, "Okay, now we're going to pray." I remember thinking, *What's worse: praying or getting a spanking?* In all those years, she never raised her voice at us. And we definitely tested her!

We can't say "Hallelujah, praise the Lord" in one breath and be explosive at home in the next. We need to act the same in church as we do at home. Our families need our emotional consistency. That starts with each other as spouses and then leads to our children.

I want to share a story with you about a safe harbor home. I like to share this story when I'm teaching on the family. It's called "The Trouble Tree."

> The carpenter I hired to help me restore an old farm house had just finished a rough first day on the job. A flat tire made him lose an hour of work, his electric saw quit, and now his ancient pickup refused to start. While he drove home, he sat in stony silence. On arriving, he invited me to meet his family. As we walked to the front door, he paused briefly at a small tree, touching the tips of the branches with both hands.
>
> When opening the door, he underwent an amazing transformation. His tanned face was wreathed in smiles

and he hugged his two small children and gave his wife a kiss. Afterward, he walked over to the car. We passed the tree, and my curiosity got the better of me. I asked him about what I had seen him do earlier.

He said, "Oh, that's my trouble tree. I know I can't help having troubles on the job, but one thing's for sure: Troubles don't belong in the house with my wife and my children. So I just hang them up on the trouble tree every night when I come home. Then in the morning I pick them up again." He smiled and added "Funny this is when I come out in the morning to pick them up, there aren't nearly as many as there were the night I hung them on the tree before."

That is the importance of providing a home that is a safe harbor. I think what this man was doing both spiritually and figuratively is a powerful exercise. We know that the Bible is very plain that we can cast our cares on God.

If I felt like there was a distance growing between my family members, I would take the kids out to eat—somewhere they wanted to go. Sometimes I would take them out one at a time, so I would have a date with my daughter and a date with my son. I would make sure I looked at them and listened to them. I didn't talk about the things I wanted to talk about. I would talk about the things they wanted to talk about.

Some people ask, "How do you do that?" Well, you learn to ask questions. You start with, "How was your day?" and they'll start talking. I know sometimes the emotional bond is lost, like when you ask a sixteen-year-old how was her day and you see her roll her eyes. But if you maintain that emotional bond as they're growing up, you can always have that connection regardless of what's going on.

Another important thing is the marriage relationship. When a husband and wife maintain an emotional bond with each other, the children see the genuine love, not the fake stuff. You can't kid your kids who live in your own house with you. All your idiosyncrasies and other stuff will come out. But when they see real love, real concern, and real connection modeled before them, I promise you they won't be able to wash it off. It'll get into their DNA.

It's also important to always emotionally separate your anger from your love from them. Don't ever discipline out of anger. Now I know parents do that, and I've made that mistake myself. But to the best you can, don't discipline out of anger.

Always remain objective with your children when negative circumstances and challenges come up. In other words, see them as who they are and the value that God has put in them. And if there's been negative circumstances or issues, deal with the issue, but do not criticize them in a way that you devalue their self-worth. Make sure that you're talking to them about who they are and how valuable they are. If there's a behavioral issue, always deal with the issue. Do not demean the value of the child in the process.

Don't live vicariously through your children. That's hard to deal with and that was hard for me. When my son and daughter were out on the field playing a sport, I wanted them to win and yelled as if I was on the field myself. I know it's hard! But don't make your kid a trophy. Celebrate the victories, but also be there in the defeats. I remember when my daughter was running for class officer and lost the election, I let her know that she was no less valuable to me whether she won or lost.

Our job as parents is not to raise good children. Our job as parents is to raise healthy adults. I want children who can grow into adulthood and be healthy, whole, and sound so that they can have a positive impact in the world.

CHAPTER 9

THE LEADER AND PRAYER

People pray in all kinds of ways. Some people pray by silently thinking and some people pray out loud. Some people get on their knees to pray, some pray in tongues, and still others pray by reciting passages or learned prayers.

In the 1980s, I watched the Jewish people pray at the Wailing Wall in Jerusalem. One thing I noticed was that they leaned forward and back as they prayed what was in their prayer books. The guide I had with me told me that the prayer book contained the Psalms from the Bible. Apparently, the Jewish people pray the same thing every day. That was so powerful to me because they are using the power of God's words to declare what Jesus said. My wife, Becky, and I learned that the words you say with your mouth are so important, and what you declare becomes your reality.

Mark 11:23 (NIV) says, *"Truly I tell you, if anyone says to this mountain, 'Go, throw yourself into the sea,' and does not doubt in their heart but believes that what they say will happen, it will be done for them."*

We knew that the act of agreement in prayer was powerful, especially between husband and wife. Becky had read a devotional about the prayer of agreement right around the time that I started traveling a lot. When I got home, we talked it over and decided we would pray together every day, no matter what. When I travel without her, we pray over the phone together and we have missed very few days, even with time differences.

God gave me and Becky a revelation with seven categories for us to pray over. I will lead us in these prayers, and Becky repeats what I pray. She doesn't just agree mentally with what I say, but she agrees with her words. Why is this important to us? Jesus says in Matthew 18:19, *"Again I say to you that if two of you agree on earth concerning anything that they ask, it will be done for them by My Father in heaven."* So we agree together in prayer that what we are asking for will be done by God.

Our seven categories for prayer:

1. Supernatural Favor

The first thing Becky and I pray for is supernatural favor. Genesis 12:2 (AMPC) says, "And I will make of you a great nation, and I will bless you [with abundant increase of favors] and make your name famous and distinguished, and you will be a blessing [dispensing good to others]."

And 2 Corinthians 9:8 (AMPC) says, "And God is able to make all grace (every favor and earthly blessing) come to you in abundance, so that you may always and under all circumstances and whatever the need be self-sufficient [possessing enough to require no aid or support and furnished in abundance for every good work and charitable donation]."

Supernatural favor is a promise of God, and we believe it is our inheritance. We already thank God for the favor in our lives, even if it hasn't shown up yet. See, God can plant dreams in our hearts as seeds, but we have to water them to make them grow. Prayer is that water.

There's an old saying, "Rome wasn't built in a day," and your dreams won't be either. The place between where we are and where we want to be is a trial of faith, and prayer is the catalyst that gets you from point A to point B. This is the part where most people give up, but if you thank God in advance for what you do not yet have, you water the seed and strengthen your faith.

Becky and I speak supernatural favor over our lives because we believe what we say with our mouths has power. We also believe that when we declare it, we are speaking favor over our lives. Psalm 5:12 (NIV) says, *"Surely Lord, you bless the righteous; you surround them with your favor as with a shield."*

God has shown us time and time again that we are favored.

2. Divine Connections

The second thing we pray for is divine connections. This refers to people we've never met and experiences we've never had. This prayer is based on the Isaiah 43:4 (Common English Bible), *"Because you are precious in my eyes, you are honored, and I love you. I give people in your place, and nations in exchange for your life."*

Years ago, I was on vacation with my wife in Hong Kong, and we stayed at an amazing spa. Our deck overlooked Victoria Harbor, and it was close enough to the shore that we could hear the lapping of the waves.

During our stay, I found an old bookstore. I began thumbing through random books and came across this quote by English publisher and philanthropist Felix Dennis: "I was put on earth to get rich, to collect the money that already had my name on it, and then give it all away." *Wow,* was all I could think!

Finding this quote in Hong Kong was a divine connection for me. I began my career as a pastor, and after meeting a successful minister who said he'd be broke in ninety days without his ministry I knew something had to change. I continued to work as a pastor, but also began aggressively investing in real estate and businesses. Before long, I was able to replace the income from my job with income produced from my assets. I was proud of myself, and I enjoyed the place my life was in at that point.

However, that quote was a divine connection because I realized that everything I was doing to pursue wealth was to build bigger barns for myself. God showed me that I could use my wealth to help others. That is why I founded my nonprofit organizations, Wealth-Builders and Tricord Global. Now, I am able to help others use their wealth to make a Kingdom impact around the globe.

God shows no favoritism, and what He will do for me, He will do for you. God constantly provides divine connections for Becky and me, bringing people into our lives who can educate and help us, whether business partners, employees, or friends.

I work with Andrew Wommack Ministries and Charis Bible College. Paul Milligan, the CEO, was an old friend of mine, and when he saw that they needed help at Andrew Wommack Ministries International (AWMI), he gave me a call. Originally, I told him no because I was retired, but my wife scolded me into calling him back. She actually told me kiddingly, "If you don't get off that couch, I might kill you!" So, I called Paul back and took a consulting position with AWMI and Charis. To say that this has been a divine connection in my life is putting it lightly.

God has divine connections for your life who will help you along the path that God has set out for you. I encourage you to believe that and pray it with me.

3. *Kairos* Moments

The third thing we pray for is similar to divine connections—*kairos* moments. *Kairos* is a Greek word meaning *decisive* and *opportune moments*. Becky and I think of it as God-opportune moments, or moments that God has orchestrated in our favor.

There is a treasure chest that God has for you, and until you begin to get a revelation of *kairos* moments, you won't be ready to receive the treasure. You don't have to go looking for those moments, just simply steward the season God has you in and be faithful to that. Be faithful in your prayer. At the same time say, "Okay, God, I'm open to whatever you are working in me, and the kairos moments you have for me." Keep your eyes open and the Holy Spirit will begin to bring things to your life.

I am convinced that we miss the kairos moments and the divine connections of our life because we aren't practiced at receiving what God is saying. When you release what's in your hand, God releases what's in His hand. In His hands are the kairos moments and divine connections that He has for you. You and I cannot afford to not obey God. There are too many treasure chests of what God has planned for your life and for the Kingdom for you and I not to be obedient in that arena.

4. Overcoming Blessings

Isaiah 45:3 says, *"I will give you the treasures of darkness and hidden riches of secret places, that you may know that I, the Lord, who call you by your name, am the God of Israel."*

5. Strategic Plans

This prayer is inspired in part by Daniel 6:3, which reads, "Then this Daniel distinguished himself above the governors and satraps, because an excellent spirit was in him; and the king gave thought to setting him over the whole realm."

6. The Double Double

Isaiah 61:7 (AMP) says, "*Instead of your [former] shame you will have a **double portion**; and instead of humiliation your people will shout for joy over their portion. Therefore in their land they will **possess double** [what they had forfeited]; everlasting joy will be theirs.*"

We pray double double over everything in our lives. We pray it over our giving, our income, our partners, and our business. The principle of double double is that God will repay you in full what was lost.

The story of Job is so compelling because it's a story of bad things that happen to a good man, and the Bible says that God allowed the suffering to come onto Job. However, when it is all over, this is what the Lord promises: "*After Job had prayed for his friends, the Lord restored his fortunes and gave him twice as much as he had before*" (Job 42:10 NIV).

As a pastor, I learned that if anything shows up in the Bible more than once, it is especially important to God. The idea of double double is no different. Whatever you have been through in your life, I can promise you that it is nothing compared to the treasures God has for you.

7. Perfect Health

Isaiah 53:5 describes the sacrifice Jesus made for us and the healing that is found in Him, "*But He was wounded for our transgressions,*

He was crushed for our wickedness [our sin, our injustice, our wrong-doing]; the punishment [required] for our well-being fell on Him, and by His stripes (wounds) we are healed."

We pray the Word of God over our bodies, that every part from our toes to our temples will be touched by perfect health. We pray away anything that threatens this for us—disease, injury, and anything else.

When my friend was battling cancer, we found a little book titled, *Healed of Cancer* by Dodie Osteen. Diagnosed with liver cancer, Dodie was told she had only three weeks to live. In her book, she gave us the recipe for getting healed. She showed us how to model her behavior and how to get what we needed from God. My friend did what she did, and he got the same results!

The real question in the case of Dodie Osteen was not how long she could live, but how well she could act until her healing manifested itself. She set an amazing example for us as believers who desire change. Thanks to her, my friend had the recipe for healing, and it worked for him too!

When I retired, I had this sensation of getting older. I didn't have to work so I spent most of my time on the couch, and I felt that in my body. Well, I read Psalm 103:5 (AMP) again and got encouraged. It says, *"Who satisfies your years with good things, so that your youth is renewed like the [soaring] eagle."* I had a revelation that God can renew my youth! I un-retired and got back to doing things I am passionate about. I watch my grandkids play baseball, and I am able to be a healthy grandfather for them.

Becky and I pray perfect health over friends, family, and others alike. We truly believe you can pray sickness away; in fact, we've seen it several times! That's why praying for perfect health is so important to us.

After we finish praying for perfect health, I stop leading the prayers and Becky starts. She leads prayers about our family, our team, our partners, and others. I agree with her in the key phrases of her prayer. I follow her the way she followed me. This is where we can get into specific needs or specific things we would like to pray for.

These seven categories have helped me be a better leader in my household, in my business, and in life. You read and learned earlier in the book that to be an effective leader, you need to be prepared. Prayer is how you can prepare yourself for the uncertainty of life. In fact, I encourage you to pray to be a better leader! Develop a habit of prayer in your life and see how drastically you can change for the better!

PART THREE

LEADERSHIP AND YOUR ORGANIZATION

CHAPTER 10

THE LEADER AND MANAGEMENT

The Leader Manager

My career started with me serving as a minister in a local church. I discovered a lot of things in those early days about people and about the principles of organization.

One thing that I noticed about people is that it is very difficult to make someone do what needs to be done when they do not want to do it. The old axiom, "You can lead a horse to water but you can't make him drink" holds true when dealing with people.

The other thing I discovered is that systems and processes that are present in many medium to large businesses and institutions seemed to be absent in small businesses, churches, and nonprofits. So not only was it necessary to learn how to lead people, but I discovered that I had to build systems from scratch. My pet peeve is when people who are in these types of businesses or organizations run out and read everything they can on leadership, when it is the systems and processes to lead the people that are missing.

In his book, *The E-Myth Revisited,* Michael E. Gerber classifies those leading small businesses and organizations into three categories: the entrepreneur, the manager, and the technician. I have my own classification system: the leader, the manager, and the doer. The focus of this book you're reading is obviously on the leader, but we also need to talk about the manager. Gerber makes the case that the entrepreneur, the leader, should be working *on* his business not *in* his business.

The concept of working on your business is one that I understood early in my career, long before I had ever read Gerber's book. But what I did not know was how to do it. I saw that the lack of systems and processes was the missing key, so I began studying how to build systems in an organization. Most small business and nonprofit leaders focus on leadership to the exclusion of any teaching on management and how to build systems. They use phrases like, "I'm not a micro manager" as though that is a valid excuse to ignore the lack of systems or management in their organization.

Within the last week of writing this chapter, I was in a large dental office and it was hopping with people. There was a very exact system in place for bringing each person into their practice as a patient. The staff was professional but also very warm and friendly. Even the dentist had time to talk to me about my needs in a warm and friendly way. I noticed while I was in the office that he was dealing with four or five different patients all in different dentist chairs at the same time. But each chair had a dental assistant who was with the patients the entire time.

The dentist drilled the hole where the cavity was, but the dental assistant did the filling. I never felt like I was not getting good service. As I was leaving, I picked up a brochure and noticed it was a dental franchise. I saw the dentist again and asked him about why he had a franchise since he was a doctor of dentistry. He said, "I know what to do to be a good dentist, but I'm pretty clueless on how to run a profitable dental practice."

This dentist had the appropriate leadership skills to hold his position, but he needed assistance with the management side of things. The franchise offered him a solution to this. However, franchising isn't the only way forward. If you are a solo leader of an organization, at the end of the day, you are generally responsible for what happens within your organization. You are responsible for what gets done and what does not get done. But sometimes, despite your best efforts, things just don't seem to progress. You feel like a cross-country runner on an asphalt road under a hot Texas sun. The road is sticky. You expend a lot of energy, but momentum is slow and draining.

What's going on? You examine your product or service and everything seems to be fine. So then you take a look at your team and see no need for change. But still, your organization is not flourishing. So, what is wrong?

The answer is simple: perhaps, you are.

No matter what sort of organization you're running—church, nonprofit, for-profit, etc., just remember that you are generally responsible for what happens in your organization. And the answer to helping your organization flourish is to make sure that you are providing the *two elements only you can provide*. These two elements ensure forward momentum. They both inspire and empower your team to get to work. These two elements produce vision and the system to bring that vision to life. So what are the two elements?

Number one is *leadership*.

Number two is *management*.

Leadership and management are powerful forces in any organization. They enable it to move forward to reach its objective efficiently. To be successful, you—the boss, founder, pastor, whatever—must be both a leader *and* a manager. It is only as you serve your people in both capacities that your organization will move toward your goals.

However, there are some who are the head of an organization or leading a team in the organization who bring neither leadership nor management. They are simply doers. The doer is what the E-Myth refers to as a technician. A doer is never able to position himself or herself to engage in leading or managing because the doer is too busy doing the work. The doer has never learned how to work through others to get something done. The doer must intentionally reposition himself or herself to carry out the role of a leader manager.

Through leadership people become unified. They develop consciousness of a kind and become committed to a cause. This commitment motivates them to readily accept new challenges and new responsibilities.

Management enables people to work together because it either acquires or builds the systems that are needed. When the system is in place, the manager makes sure the system is operating fully. Individual efforts are coordinated into team efforts within the system. When faced with a challenge, the team is ready to go to work because they know how to work and how to get the job done efficiently and harmoniously.

If you want your organization to be successful, supply your people with both leadership and management. Both responsibilities are demanding in time and energy. You already know that it takes a great deal of time and energy to be the organization's leader.

It is only as you serve your people in both capacities that your organization will move toward your objectives.

The terms *leader* and *manager* are used in many ways, so before we move forward, let's define our terms.

A *manager* concentrates more on work than on people. A manager operates within established patterns and practices. The manager gets the job done by directing and guiding the work of others within the limits of those practices. Since the manager is more focused on the work, the role is more *transactional*.

A *leader* concentrates more on people than on work. A leader moves people out of the limits of the traditional. He enables people to move into new areas of activity and achievement. A leader does this not by direct control, but through the relationship he or she has with the team. A leader is *transformational*.

Good parents have learned their job is not to raise good children but to raise good adults. To help a child grow and mature and to prevent harm from coming to the child, a parent at times must be very transactional, like a manager. At other times a parent should be transformational by inspiring and bonding with their children.

I once heard someone say that leadership is essentially a "relationship between individuals—between the leader and every member of the group he leads." Leadership inspires people. It makes them *want* to work.

Management, on the other hand, provides the know-how, the sound planning, and the means for stability in an organization. It enables people to reach the objectives inspired by leadership.

Balance Is Necessary

Both leadership and management are essential in the work of any dynamic organization. If the manager is the head of the organization, the leader is the heart. Nowhere is the balance between leader and manager more important than in the person leading the organization.

The people of your organization require a sense of mission. They must have inspiration to become involved in the work of the organization. Leadership supplies this inspiration. Without leadership, morale will falter.

However, people also want—and need—direction and guidance for how to fulfill the mission. Without providing clear direction, morale also falters. Other people in your organization, no matter how capable they are, simply cannot satisfy these two needs.

History is full of people who have experimented with delegating one or the other of these two responsibilities to a subordinate. It usually hasn't worked. Why? Because delegating one of these important roles requires an organization to have two heads. Jesus, the master Teacher, said, *"No one can serve two masters"* (Matthew 6:24 NIV).

Each organization and each section *within* an organization must have one person who is ultimately responsible for motivating the team and coordinating their efforts. This person can delegate many duties but not the top leadership and management responsibilities. To do so creates problems within the organization.

Learn from a Football Coach

Let's compare the key person's role to that of a football coach. Consider Bill Belichick of the American football team, the New England Patriots. He has won more Super Bowls than any other coach. He is an excellent leader *and* an excellent manager. He has demonstrated how one person can propel an organization to great success.

When Belichick was approached about coaching the Patriots, he said he would accept the job offer under one condition: he would be the coach *and* the general manager.

Belichick knew a successful football organization could have only one leader. He was a man who had direct control over all phases of the operation. In this way, he was able to move the team's efforts in one direction, toward one specific goal.

Belichick also knew how to select the right talent. He knew football inside and out and was able to communicate his knowledge to his team. He formulated game plans and was able to effectively use his players' talents to win. In fact when some of his star players were injured and could not play, he would just plug another player in and the team performed flawlessly.

Like Belichick, every good manager must know how to do three things:

1. Select the right people.

2. Train the right people.

3. Use the right people's talents in the most efficient way to get the job done.

But Belichick is more than a manager. He is also a leader. He brings out the best in each player. He inspires them week after week. His players always seem to give him their best. They want to win for him as well as for themselves. This type of leadership has caused them to win championships year after year.

Again, like Belichick, every good leader must know how to do three things:

1. Empower the right people to be the best they can be.

2. Envision a goal for the right people.

3. Inspire the right people to achieve that goal.

When the key person of an organization combines these six traits, momentum will really start to accelerate.

Leadership without Management

What happens if you offer your team leadership or management, but not both?

If you provide only leadership, the morale of the group will remain high for a while. But without direction, people lose sight of the objective and tend to be distracted by unnecessary tangents. They fail to move together toward the organization's goals. They might be working hard, but nothing really happens.

The members of the organization can feel that something is wrong. They aren't getting anywhere. They need someone to coordinate their work. We all know people who have real leadership qualities but possess little management ability. People love them but only for a while. These leaders generate dozens of new ideas but they lack the discipline to bring them to completion. Before one idea is executed, they are off to the next.

This type of leader tends to send up a lot of fireworks. There is a moment of beautiful display. Everyone marvels at the wonderful ideas. However, because there is no one present to execute the ideas, nothing of significance happens. The interest of the team lags in such a situation. Eventually, they look for someone who can manage their efforts *and* help them achieve their goals.

Management without Leadership

What about the person with management skills but no leadership? When the focus is strictly on management, morale may not even have the chance to get started. You can organize every little thing and provide a plethora of plans and well-engineered programs. But without leadership, the effort is wasted.

In this scenario, the members of your organization can feel uninspired. Everything is laid out for them, but they aren't given the vision or the purpose. People don't often *love* managers the way they do leaders. With management, everything is cut and dry. With leadership, everything is vibrant colors. Your people need both.

Managers can write the playbook, but they are not the ones delivering the inspiring pre-game, rev-everybody-up speech that the coach gives. Again, the interest of the team lags. In this scenario, the interest might never even be hooked. Eventually, the team members will look for someone who can inspire them.

Improving as a Leader

Until picking up this book, you might not have thought of your role as being both the manager and the leader. Do you think you are doing a good job in both areas? Or do you need improvement?

You *can* improve as a leader. There is quite a bit of uncertainty on the subject of leadership, because it is somewhat intangible. It can be hard to pinpoint the exact reason why some people are leaders and others are not, no matter how they try. This causes some people to believe that leaders are born and not made.

It is true that certain people have qualities—such as self-confidence, enthusiasm, or personal charisma—that help them emerge as leaders faster than others. However, if you don't naturally possess these qualities, it does not mean that you are doomed as a leader. You can work on yourself to develop these qualities.

Two Basic Ingredients

There are two basic ingredients always found in strong leaders. The first is *connection*. The leader builds connection with the team by identifying with them and allowing them to identify with him or her in return. There is a reciprocal bond when this relationship is felt by both a leader and the followers.

A leader must always know the people. He or she must be aware of their dreams, hopes, fears, and their feelings of inadequacy. The world's greatest leaders enjoyed the devoted support of their followers. Why? It's because they identified with their followers. They lived the same way, ate the same food, and shared the same hopes, dreams, experiences, dangers, and discomforts.

Certainly a leader is entitled to some privileges but too many leaders become greedy. They want too many privileges and become proud and distant. People are no longer able to identify with them, so they start to disconnect. When his happens, the leader just becomes a boss instead of a leader. This greed inhibits his or her ability to inspire. That is why it is necessary for a true leader to build and maintain a connection with his or her team.

The second leadership ingredient is *communication*. The leader must be able to communicate with members of the team as a group, as well as with individuals within the group. In the same way, it's important that the team members know that the leader is listening to them. Team members should always feel as though they will get a fair hearing for their ideas, fears, and dreams.

In turn, the leader must be able to communicate to team members a sense of hope and assurance: hope that their desires can be realized and assurance that their problems will be solved.

Communication takes time. Unless you are willing to take the time to be with your people—to listen to them and speak to them—you will never really be the leader. Therefore, to improve your position as a leader, you must improve your communication skills.

One fundamental part of communication is the ability to listen effectively. The axiom that says, "People don't care how much you know until they know how much you care" certainly applies when we are talking about communication.

Improving as a Manager

Just as you can improve as a leader, you can also improve as a manager. The word *management* was coined by the Romans and was first applied to hand-training wild horses. The Romans believed that there were many jobs man could do better by utilizing the energy of horses.

For example, if the job called for moving a large quantity of material, a manager could use horses to move larger loads faster. Or if the job required someone to move from one place to another, he could move faster and farther by using horsepower. This, of course, meant that the man had to size up the job, select the right horse for that job, and train it to perform properly.

This was the Roman understanding of management. Over time, the word *management* evolved to describe the task of using manpower to get a job done. You can improve as a manager if you follow the same steps in utilizing manpower that the Romans used in utilizing horsepower: know how to step back and see what needs exist, know how to put systems in place to meet those needs, and know how to pick and train the right people within those systems.

Seven Steps for Improvement

The following seven steps will help you improve as the powerful leader-manager hybrid.

1. Don't try to do it all yourself. The one-man band notions himself a musician, but generally people don't gain much from his performance. He is a performer, not an artist.

2. Size up the job. Think through exactly what it is that you want to do. Define clear objectives, make plans, and write everything down on paper or on your computer screen. Then, study those objectives and plans. Make sure you know exactly what you want to do. Have an idea of how you can do it and what help you may need.

3. Provide direction in writing. Stated generally, "If it's not in writing, it doesn't count." Putting directions in writing enables those who read it to run with the idea. An Old Testament prophet wrote what the Lord said, "Write the vision and make it plain" (Habakkuk 2:2). Most people think that providing direction is just providing vision. But real direction comes not only with vision but also with clear expectations, processes, and systems—that are put in writing!

4. Select the right people. One reason so many people have difficulty managing is that they have the wrong people assisting them. You may not be able to directly select the assistance you need, but you can at least insist that they be selected on the basis of qualifications that you help to establish.

5. Establish a core dialogue schedule. Have your team report back to you on a regular schedule. Regular reporting enables the leader manager to keep track of the pulse of the organization.

6. Spend time in training. Unless people are trained for the job requirements and procedures, they will not work efficiently. No matter how willing your workers may be, if they lack training, they cannot do their tasks properly.

7. Use people wisely. Do not overwork your people, but do not underemploy them either. Use their talents and abilities wisely. To do this, you need to plan, communicate, and consult with them on work expectations—both their expectations and yours.

When you act as an effective leader *and* manager, morale in your organization will be high. Plans will move forward with greater harmony and enthusiasm. People will enjoy being part of your organization and supporting the work being done there. Best of all, your intentions will be carried out without requiring too much of your personal energy.

CHAPTER 11

THE LEADER AND PROVIDING DIRECTION

Identifying, Standardizing, and Directing Work

Systems give you more time to be a leader because they make the task of management easier. Several years ago, I encountered a frustrated senior pastor in a church where I was a guest speaker. He came into his office and slammed the door on a Sunday morning. He complained that the nursery still had dirty diapers from the week before in the dirty diaper pail. He told me how many times he had explained to the nursery leader how the nursery should be cleaned and the dirty diapers emptied.

I didn't say anything in the moment but waited to see if he would bring it up again after church was over. Sure enough, on our ride back to the airport, he brought it up once again. As he was venting, I told him, "If the direction you provide is not in writing, it doesn't count." He looked at me and immediately pulled the car over to the side of the road.

"Say that again," he said.

"If it's not in writing and people have not been given clear instruction about the expectations and standard operating procedures, then you cannot be frustrated if they have not done what you *verbally* told them."

He called me later to say how that small piece of information transformed his life. He proceeded to write job descriptions, policies, and procedures for every area of his church.

For that pastor, this was the simple beginning of having systems in his organization. For the first time, he understood the importance of clearly defined systems. Those systems enabled the work to be regulated and directed without him needing to be personally present. That freed him up immensely for the job of leading his church.

In order to systematize the work in your organization, you need to first clearly identify what work needs to be done. Then sort out and classify the various jobs that have to be done. In organizations where systematizing the work has never been done before, it becomes necessary to actually interview everyone in order to identify clearly what work is being done.

In running small businesses, there have been times when I needed to sit my team down and have them each go through everything they do on a daily and weekly schedule. This helped us to redirect our efforts in a more efficient way. Interviewing your people is the best way to get a clear picture so you can systematize accordingly.

Many of today's leadership books overemphasize the importance of being a leader to the exclusion of being a manager. There's no question that in today's world we must learn to be leaders. However, in small businesses and small organizations, the effort of identifying what work needs to be done is really part of the management process.

Many organizations become paralyzed in their ability to move forward because they have never clearly identified the work that is causing their organization to function. If you don't have a full picture of what work is being done, you have no idea what's missing or what's extraneous. Discovering those things will help you streamline the process.

Once the work has been identified, it must be standardized. *Standardizing* means to make the work that is to be done consistent, with little variation. Many have heard of the management technique called Six Sigma. It is a set of management techniques intended to improve business processes by greatly reducing the probability that an error or defect will occur. This actually happens when work is correctly standardized. Learn how to control work by directing the right amount of effort to the right job, at the right place, at the right time. Don't let work control you.

These three activities—identifying, standardizing, and directing work—are the heart and core of systems. Systems have enabled leader managers the world over to get more work done, with much less effort.

Organizations of all kinds use systems to help delegate work, supervise less, and enjoy greater results. Systems provide for better working conditions in any organization. There is less tension, and people are much happier.

How Systems Work Began

Systems work came from the scientific management movement of the early 1900s. The emphasis of that movement was primarily directed toward industrial production. Most of the scientific management techniques, attitudes, and concepts have found their way into modern organizations. In short, Scientific Management teaches: If you study work and analyze what you're doing, you will find a way to do it better and easier, and you will get greater production because you eliminate wasted effort.

Systems work is an intentional, orderly, human approach to the exercise of management responsibility. It is the opposite of the hit-or-miss approach practiced, though not recommended, in many organizations today. It's important to clarify that systems work is the study and analysis of work, not the study and analysis of people. People are involved, but the main emphasis of systems work is on the work itself. Through systems you can identify, systematize, and regulate the work.

I see leaders who read books on the subject of innovation. Then they try to bring innovation into their organization, not realizing that without systemization there is nothing to innovate. Today's message of innovation is aimed at organizations that have outdated systems and processes—in short, systems and processes that need to be innovated. Without the presence of a system, there is nothing to be innovated. Most small businesses and organizations must first *develop* systems and processes. For them, that is innovation.

Begin by Analyzing Your Own Work

To be a better leader manager, begin by analyzing your own work and systematizing your own responsibilities. To do this, you analyze and identify exactly what you do. We have already identified two distinct responsibilities: you must be a leader and a manager.

It is only when you think of these two duties as being separate and distinct, that you can begin to systematize your work and ultimately determine how much time and energy you must direct to each duty.

Two Types of Work

There are two types of work in any organization: routine and developmental. About 70 percent of the work in an organization is routine work. The other 30 percent is developmental work.

As an organization grows, almost all of the responsibilities of the manager role can be delegated. This is because the manager's role is primarily overseeing routine work.

On the other hand, the leader's role becomes more and more important as an organization grows. When the manager's role is largely delegated, the leader's role becomes 70 percent developmental work and 30 percent management work.

Development work includes study, research, forecasting, and decision making. It contains project work, unique situations, rare problems, emergencies, and addressing any gaps that come from missing goals or poor performance in general.

Developmental work is innately innovative, and therefore, difficult to systematize. The leader may use a systematic approach to developmental work, but the work itself does not lend itself to systematization.

The reason many beginning entrepreneurs purchase a franchise is because the systems, processes, and best practices have already been identified and included in the business plan. Training programs from the franchisers train the franchisees how to institute and carry out these best business practices. Franchising is basically an entrepreneur's "Easy" button. But when it comes to pure start-up, there is no preexisting manual. That manual needs to be created and that creation process is the role of management.

Delegation

The manager is in charge of ensuring that work gets done. Because there is so much work that needs to be done, managers need assistance or end up doing all the work themselves—to the point of exhaustion. It is at this point that true management—getting work done through others—bears fruit.

The manager's work is regulated by the amount of personal effort and time dedicated to it. But it is also regulated by determining how much of the work can be done through the time and efforts of others. Delegation is not a process whereby the manager abdicates his or her work responsibility! Through delegation, the manager expands his or her own efforts through the efforts of others.

Case Study

In the book of Exodus, Jethro, Moses' father-in-law, advocated delegation. Exodus 18:13-24 (AMPC) the tells us:

Next day Moses sat to judge the people, and the people stood around Moses from morning till evening. When Moses' father-in-law saw all that he was doing for the people, he said, What is this that you do for the people? Why do you sit alone, and all the people stand around you from morning till evening? Moses said to his father-in-law, Because the people come to me to inquire of God. When they have a dispute they come to me, and I judge between a man and his neighbor, and I make them know the statutes of God and His laws.

Moses' father-in-law said to him, The thing that you are doing is not good. You will surely wear out both yourself and this people with you, for the thing is too heavy for you; you are not able to perform it all by yourself. Listen now to [me]; I will counsel you, and God will be with you. You shall represent the people before God, bringing their cases and causes to Him, Teaching them the decrees and laws, showing them the way they must walk and the work they must do. Moreover, you shall choose able men from all the people—God-fearing men of truth who hate unjust gain—and place them over thousands, hundreds, fifties, and tens, to be their rulers. And let them judge the people at all times; every great matter they shall bring to you, but every small matter they shall judge. So it will be easier for you, and they will bear the burden with you. If you will do this, and God so commands you, you will be able to endure [the strain], and all these people also will go to their [tents] in peace.

So Moses listened to and heeded the voice of his father-in-law and did all that he had said.

What can we learn as we analyze Jethro's advice to Moses?

1. Jethro told Moses that he wasn't regulating his work very well, and because of this, Moses and the people were suffering (verses 17-18). Moses was zealous in the task assigned to him by the Lord, but he was burning himself out. Furthermore, the people were not being effectively served (verse 13).

2. Moses had two responsibilities (verse 20): Show them the way they must walk (leader); show them the work they must do (manager).

3. Moses was to divide his management responsibilities into two parts: great matters and small matters (verse

22). He himself was to handle the great matters (developmental work), while the smaller matters (routine work) were to be delegated.

4. Following this advice, leading became easier for Moses, and the people were able to go to their places in peace (verse 23).

Effective Systems Need Prompt Feedback

Since Moses' day, there have been improvements in the management process. One of the most significant improvements is the use of information to enable the manager to accomplish the work. In this modern era of smart phones, laptop computers, and an abundance of apps and software, obtaining information quickly has come to be expected. Properly applied, these new apps and software can give the manager all of the real-time information he or she needs to manage the organization.

The power of managers to direct work by their physical presence is limited; they can stand by the elbow of only one person at a time. To manage any appreciable quality of day-to-day routine work, managers cannot personally direct and communicate with those doing the work. They need something that will help them guide group action and get the group working together.

Remember, all work is either routine or developmental. Most all-routine work can be quantified. Just as the dashboard of a car records speed, RPMs, and gas quantity, an organization needs a dashboard of its own. In modern management, the dashboard is a management tool used to get an overview of the enterprise's health. Some software has key indicators for specific types of businesses already dash-boarded. If that's not available, a simple Excel sheet with graphs that are updated daily, weekly, or monthly will suffice. Find what works for your organization and stick with it.

Routine work can be dash-boarded so the manager can address the gaps in performance based on what the dashboard indicates. Take a sales section, for example. If sales have gone down by 20 percent over the last month, that tells the manager that the decrease in sales must be discussed at the next team meeting. In a church, if the numbers of visiting families have dropped by a high percentage over the last quarter, then it probably means that the outreach section has not been performing well. A dashboard allows managers to keep their finger on the pulse of all routine work that must be carried out for the organization to be successful and effective.

Developmental work can best be carried out using some type of project management software. Remember this type of work is difficult to systematize and has a newness about it that can best be kept track of using project management techniques.

Characteristics of a System

1. A system is made up of a number of parts.

2. All parts are interconnected, and each part is essential to the whole.

3. There is a sequential pattern to the activity of the parts.

4. The action of each part influences the action of all other parts.

5. Activity and information flow through the parts, galvanizing, empowering, and enabling them to accomplish a specific purpose.

6.   The leader manager controls the system by monitoring the flow of information and activity, and then providing feedback and direction as needed.

What Causes a System to Fail

Basically, there are four causes of failure: people, information, design, and direction:

1.   People

- People do not know what to do.

- People are not properly motivated.

- People are not properly selected.

2.   Information

- Lack of information.

- Faulty information.

- Excessive or unnecessary information.

3.   Design

- Improper design—the leader manager must eliminate tension where the different parts intersect.

- No design—design the system for what is needed.

4.   Direction

- Scarcity of direction.

- Extreme direction.

The Principle Job Description of a Leader Manager

The following is a general job description of a leader manager who will succeed in reaching goals:

1. Set measurable standards, and let everyone know what is expected of them.

2. Establish checkpoints.

3. Measure performance and progress. Constantly monitor the system.

4. Evaluate these measurements.

5. Redirect action as necessary.

CHAPTER 12

THE LEADER AND SYSTEMS

Planned Systems Work Better

Whether you are aware of it or not, your organization currently has systems. It has activity and work going on at all times. That activity can be planned or it can be unplanned. Both a planned system and an unplanned system get work done. But there's a vast difference in the degree of effort required with one type of system over the other. In most unplanned systems, effort goes down the drain over time.

Consider the personal expertise required to guide a barge down the winding Mississippi River. Mississippi River pilots have difficulty seeing around the bend and avoiding the shallows. Compare that effort with the labor required to guide that same vessel in straight waterway of the right depth. Obviously, it is much easier and more effective to guide the ship in the straight channel of the appropriate depth.

We do need to work hard, but we also need to work efficiently. The Bible tells us that God is not the author of confusion. It also says that

He would have all things done decently and in order (see 1 Corinthians 14:33, 40).

The apostle Paul tells us in 1 Corinthians 12:28 that God has placed some in the church with the gift of administration. The Greek word used here for administration is *kybérnēsis*, which literally means helmsman. The helmsman controls the ship. He plans its course of action and directs it accordingly. He does not let the ship wander as the wind may blow it; he steers it along a prescribed course.

Jesus Planned

In the story of the feeding of the 5,000, the Bible says that Jesus commanded the disciples to make the crowd sit down in groups upon the green grass. They sat down in ranks, by hundreds and by fifties. We also know that when He sent forth the seventy on the first missionary expedition, He arranged for them to go in pairs. Jesus did things in an orderly fashion. He used planned work cycles to get the job done efficiently.

A planned organizational system helps you do the same thing. In your business or in your church, it enables you to use all the available resources, such as people, time, money, and equipment to achieve your goals more efficiently.

Systems are what a leader manager directs. Sometimes, someone else provides the leader manager with the necessary systems, but sometimes the leader manager must build the systems. Most entrepreneurs and church leaders have to provide or create the systems themselves. Now I'm going to give leader managers a start to creating the systems they need in their organizations to be effective and successful. So let's get started.

Management is the science of getting people to contribute their best efforts to work that needs to be done. This implies that you as a leader manager know what work people need to do. You must communicate who is going to do the work and how it will be done. You may have to determine when and where people do the work. At times you will have to explain to them why the work must be done.

As a leader manager, you must establish an environment in which people can and will work together harmoniously. Any leader, whether a business owner, a start-up entrepreneur, or a leader of a nonprofit, must understand how to be both a leader and manager.

What Is a System?

A system is a single entity made up of two or more component parts. Each individual part has a definite relationship to every other part. The action of any one part has a direct effect on the action of every other part. Therefore to function smoothly, a system must be well-designed and controlled.

An organizational system is comprised of different people parts. Someone needs to be in charge of *coordinating* the *work relationships* of these people so they cooperate with one another as *individuals* or as *groups* to get the *job* done. That someone is the manager.

Please note my emphasis on the terms *work, job, coordinating, relationships, individuals,* and *groups.* These words are foundational to understanding the leader manager's job.

Every organization has a job to do. If it is going to get that job done effectively, a leader manager is needed to enable people to develop good working relationships. An understanding of systems will simplify the responsibility of this organizational manager.

Thus, a system must be defined as an organizational management tool for bringing the people parts of an organization together and forming them into a well-coordinated working unit.

A system may be small, or it may be large. It may be a single unit, or it may be a composite of a number of smaller units.

Take a car engine, for example. The entire collection of nuts, bolts, wires, springs, and valves all make up the mechanical system. Even the driver, by engaging the ignition and placing a foot on the accelerator, becomes part of the system.

But the mechanical system of the car is a composite of the smaller subsystems within the car's mechanical system, such as the fuel system, electrical system, and transmission system.

Each of the subsystems needs to function smoothly and be coordinated with every other system if the total mechanical system is to fulfill its purpose—getting the driver safely to the destination.

Systems are important not only in the area of mechanical systems, but also in the area of people group systems.

The Formation of Groups

Since the beginning of time, people have been rubbing shoulders with one another in groups. Groups are formed in many ways and for many reasons. A crowd of people standing on the street corner waiting for the signal to change is one kind of group. The fans gathered together in a football stadium and the passengers in the jet flying at 29,000 feet are also groups.

These groups, however, are temporary in nature. The members come together in a casual way for a short while and then they disperse. Although they may have a common purpose in the moment, they are not actively working with one another to achieve a goal. There is little structure in such groups. All members may step off the curb when the light changes or sit in assigned seats in the stadium while the teams are playing, but otherwise, they demonstrate little organization.

There are, however, groups that are more enduring in nature, possessing more organization. These groups work together to achieve a goal, and therefore, require more structure. These are the groups we will be focusing on as all organizations are made up of these groups.

Examine an organization, and you will discover that there is a lot of activity going on within it. This activity will *hopefully* enable the organization to accomplish its purpose and reach its objectives. But *implementing* systems *will* enable this organization to manage its people groups, and therefore, reach its plans, goals, and objectives.

The Relationship between Systems and Activity

There is a relationship between systems and activity. To understand what the relationship between organizational activity and systems is, let's look at a typical manufacturing firm. It is organized around sections or departments. There is a purchasing section, a production section, a finance section, etc.

Examine each section and you will see individuals working. In one office, for example, someone will be working on the computer handling invoices. Meanwhile in another section, someone is taking care of purchasing materials. At the same time, someone else in another section is handling human resources. The assembly line is all the while operating with many more activities. If you were to observe long enough, you would see that all of these different activities are connected.

Effectiveness depends on how well all of these individual people and sections are connected. A system connects all of the various sections and work cycles into one cohesive group. This group can then move forward in order to accomplish the organizational objectives.

As you examine the entire organization, section by section, you will also discover that every individual's activities are linked to the activities of every other individual. Not only are the *individual* activities connected, the *departmental* activities are also connected.

Activity within the finance section is directly related to activity within the production section—which is related to activity within the purchasing section. All of these smaller systems are tied together to make the total organizational system.

In addition to the work systems within any organization, there are also social systems. For example, there are activities that tie people together in social relationships. The very first human organization and its social and works system is found in the book of Genesis. In Genesis 2:18, we read that the Lord God said, *"It is not good that man should be alone; I will make him a helper comparable to him."* Adam and Eve were supposed to be companions to each other. They formed a social subsystem within the greater system of marriage but also constituted a work subsystem as they helped each other with tasks.

Likewise, every human organization today is made up of a network of social systems and work systems. Wise managers in business have learned that they must have plans to tie all of these subsystems together.

An understanding of systems planning enables leader managers to coordinate all activity within an organization so that they are able to get all workers and all the sections to pull in the same direction. It is that coordinated pull that permits an organization to reach its goals efficiently with the least amount of expenditure in time, effort, and money. Without a planned system, the activity of any organization is fraught with misguided energy and bumbling inefficiency.

A system is valuable in any organization. A system does not in and of itself make a profit, but it does empower an organization—which obviously needs to make a profit to survive—to make a profit. In an organization, such as a church, which is not designed to make a profit, a system results in better performance and greater ability to reach goals and objectives.

A System Does Not Operate Itself

A system does not operate by itself. It needs competent people to plan and run it. The leader manager is the key figure in making a system work. Such a person must understand the principles of organization, planning, and organizational control.

You cannot get the maximum performance out of people without being organized. You need planned and controlled activities. Having a planned system enables a leader manager to be successful in reaching goals.

Through a system, the leader manager allocates responsibilities, making use of the best available skills and fitting them together into a workable plan so that the work gets done in the best possible manner. This avoids chaos and confusion by coordinating all activity within an organization.

It is naïve to think that logical plans develop by themselves. Logical plans are the result of concentrated, intelligent effort. It is equally naïve to think that people can automatically synchronize their efforts into an efficient working plan. They need assistance and guidance to do so.

Systems Are the Answer

The organizational system primarily provides that assistance by providing information people need to work together efficiently.

After a leader manager approves a work plan for the organization, there needs to be a method for telling people how they fit into that plan, what they must do to carry out that plan, and *how* they must do it. The leader manager also needs some method to receive information back to know how well the work is proceeding so necessary action can be taken to further improve the work efforts of his team. The organizational system, with its related processes, procedures, reporting and more, accomplishes all of these needs.

Leader managers learned a long time ago that passing information along verbally is generally unreliable. It is much better to communicate direction and expectations in writing since people can read and retain better than just listening. There's an old proverb that says, "Spoken words fly away, written words remain." People need clear, written direction in order to get work done properly.

People can easily forget or confuse verbal direction, but written direction can be referred to again and again. Therefore, as a leader manager, you would be wise to learn how to use written direction to:

1. Tell people about plans.

2. Tell each person how he or she can contribute to the plan.

3. Tell each person what others are also doing to contribute to the plan.

4. Obtain information on how the work is proceeding so you can redirect the action as necessary.

A leader manager can be an entrepreneur, business owner, non-profit leader, or anyone who needs to get something accomplished with the help of others. With that understanding, management is best defined as the art of getting work done through others.

The job of working through other people is never easy. Have you ever heard a person say they would rather do it than take the time to tell someone else how to do it? What is that person really saying? Basically that the job of working through other people—the act of tying efforts together into an efficient unit—is work itself.

The person who gets other people to work together uses a lot of energy. It's called leader manager energy! There is planning involved. There is providing direction to others so they can do the work. And then there is inspecting the work to see that it gets done properly. All of this activity and energy is work itself and takes a great deal of time.

Remember that leading any organization requires both art and science. Learning how to lead an organization as a leader manager is a process like eating. You can only eat so much at one time. So it must be with your efforts to understand and build systems as a leader manager—you can only do so much at once. Take bite-sized chunks. Remember the well-known proverb, "How do you eat a whale? One bite at a time."

CHAPTER 13

THE LEADER AND ORGANIZING

Charting Your Organization

When your organization was first formed, the reason for its existence, the *raison d'tere,* was clear in everyone's mind. Everyone who connected with the organization in its infancy knew its reason for being. When sections were organized, they were organized to help the parent organization meet its purpose. All activity was in proper perspective.

As time passes, as people come and go, the perspective may get out of focus. This is commonly known as "mission drift." Often, the people who originally provided the support activity forget that their work is support work. They begin to think that what *they* do is the *raison d'etre* of the organization. Their efforts began to overshadow the original purpose of the group.

Many years ago, I witnessed a board member of a church shut down one of the church's primary outreaches. The children who attended this particular outreach came on Saturday morning and made it necessary for the janitor to come and clean the church twice a week. Instead of asking the janitor to clean once a week on

Saturday afternoon, the entire outreach was eliminated. In an effort to cut costs in one area, a key church activity was shut down, thus harming the church's mission.

To prevent things like this from happening, businesses need to continually be reminded of their purpose. Refocusing again and again on the *raison d'etre* highlights key activities of the business so each is accurately identified and supported. One of the failures of small businesses is not taking the time to properly identify the key work bundles that are necessary to deliver their value proposition. Just identifying and systematizing those work bundles correctly allows the small business to grow.

Large corporations, on the other hand, can become so bureaucratic with inefficient systems that they have stopped delivering value to the customer. They have lost touch with what the contemporary customer is expecting or demanding. This is when innovation becomes crucial to the business's survival. Change is introduced, key activities are again identified, and the work is rebundled to deliver what the contemporary customer is expecting.

How to Use an Organization Chart

The leader manager uses an organization chart as an aid to thoughts. The picture that the organization chart draws allows the leader manager to reflect and ask the question, *Is this structure the best for the work that needs to be done? Have I grouped the work efficiently so the most work with the least amount of effort can be accomplished?*

When thinking about the work bundles, the leader manager should consider subordinates and their effectiveness. Have the work bundles been properly identified and directed?

There are seven key questions that the leader manager can ask at this point:

1. Is this part of my organization too big?

2. Is it out of balance with the other parts of my organization?

3. Is the work that needs to be done organized in the best way?

4. Are two or more jobs so closely related that I should consider having them made into a single function?

5. Is the responsibility emphasis, as reflected on this chart, the correct emphasis? Is it right for our main objectives?

6. Are we over-organized in some areas?

7. Does the complexity of our work require a more complex organization?

People throughout the organization can also use the chart to help them understand how the organization works and the role they play as individuals. It also helps them to understand the authority pattern. How does all the work activity link up? Who has the responsibility for doing a certain job? The chart should include all of this information.

When people know the answers to these questions, they can expedite their own work. They can reach the right person at the right time on the right subject. This helps everyone in the organization. Charts also help new people orient themselves to the organization's structure. Sure, they will figure it out eventually, but why let them stumble through the first few weeks when an organization chart can speed up the process?

LEADERSHIP **MASTERY**

These are just some of the benefits that come from the use of organizational charts. Perhaps you have thought of other ways that charts can be of specific value to your organization. Well, before you put this book down and start sketching one out, we have some groundwork to cover!

Begin by writing down the purpose of your organization. Articulate this clearly. People are much more likely to support something when you let them know what it is. As the Lord said in Habakkuk 2:2 (New Living Translation), *"Write my answer plainly on tablets, so that a runner can carry the correct message to others."* The purpose of the organization should be understood clearly in the minds of all who are part of it.

Identify the Work Bundles

Next, ascertain the work bundles of the activities of your organization. If you are a small business owner, list all of the primary jobs that you are doing right now in your business. Even if you have a few employees, the responsibility for most of the major tasks of your business falls on you. Examples of key activities that can be grouped into work bundles are accounting, marketing, legal, human resources, information technology, operations, etc.

If you are the pastor of a church, some of your key activities may be preaching, music, outreach, prayer ministry, missions, youth, children, finance, etc.

Once you have listed every key activity you can think of, arrange them into logical work bundles. For example, all work relating to finances goes into one bundle. All work relating to marketing goes into another work bundle.

Typically in the church, all work relating to children's ministry goes into one work bundle, and all work relating to missions goes into another bundle.

The most important thing to remember—*all work bundles on an organization chart represent function, not people.* Let me say that one more time. Work bundles boxes that are drawn on an organization chart are not drawn with people in mind; they are drawn to represent function.

In your charting, concentrate on the work and not on the people. Usually your work bundles will remain relatively stable. There will always be somebody in charge of the work, but it is not always the same person. People come and go. So, on your chart, place the major emphasis on the work, not the individuals. Even on your main chart, the work title and the key spot should not be the name of the person who is president. Rather, it is the title "president."

With this understanding in mind, make work titles dominate your chart. Give these titles prominence by putting each at the top of the box. In fact, show them in bold letters. Remember that the person in the box is transient, so put that name in smaller type. Team members are temporary occupants. A certain person may be responsible for the work today but may not be in that position tomorrow.

For titles, choose words that mean something. When you do that, your chart shows basic work responsibilities. The chart becomes more than just a picture of the organizational structure. It is a summary of all major work assignments.

What the Organization Chart Shows

A well-constructed organization chart shows four primary aspects:

1. The primary functions of the organization (the work bundles)

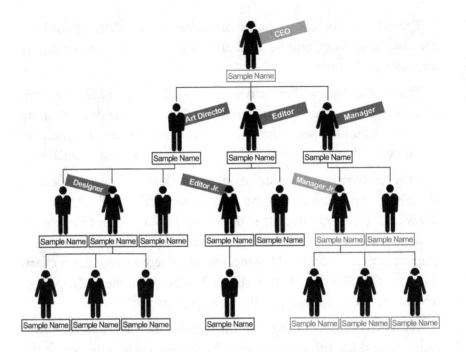

2. The title of the position

3. The person's name who is responsible for the work bundles

4. Lines that connect the boxes to show the lines of authority and accountability

Inside each box, the primary function or work bundles should be in the largest font. The title of the position should be in the second largest font. The person's name who is responsible should be in the smallest font.

A Cautionary Note

Do not be afraid of the details. There was a buzzword back in the 1990s—micromanagement. The idea was that real leaders never get bogged down in micromanagement. In other words, real leaders never get into the "weeds;" they let others go there. The advice was to focus on leadership and the big picture and not get swamped with details. For those who are in higher positions, this is great advice.

However, this advice was written primarily to those who are working in an established corporate culture and structure. Typically in established corporate structures, systems are already in place. Even if the systems are archaic, they're in place. Therefore, the executive role is not to establish the system but to merely improve upon it or administrate it in a more effective way. In fact, history is littered with successful corporate executives who left their established corporate structures to start their own businesses. And then those businesses failed miserably. Those executives were incredibly effective when the system had been provided for them but struggled mightily when they had to develop their own systems.

Entrepreneurs who are starting businesses from scratch or pastors who are pastoring small-to-medium-sized churches do not have the luxury of a pre-established corporate structure. They must create one from nothing. That is why it is so important to know how to correctly develop an organization chart.

Without getting too far into the weeds, real leadership is providing an organization chart if your business or church or other organization does not have one. This is also true if the current chart is out of date. And for many large, established organizations, clarifying and updating the organization chart is part of the innovation process. This is why knowing how to create an organizational chart is a key skill for any leader manager.

How to Create an Organization Chart

An organization chart is a language of its own. To make it readable for other people, the language must be consistent. To communicate consistently, set up sensible standards and stick with them. Here's a summary of organization chart standards:

1. Show the date that the chart was created. I usually place the date in the top right-hand corner of the chart.

2. Emphasize the key function—work group—that is being charted by placing it in the largest box. Use the largest font on the chart to identify the work group being charted.

3. Use medium-size rectangle boxes aligned horizontally under the key box to represent the functions that report to the key function box.

4. Use small rectangular boxes aligned vertically under the medium-sized boxes to show all primary functions necessary to form the work group in the medium-sized boxes.

5. Use thick lines to connect the boxes.

6. Write a function in each box.

7. Next in the box, show the position title of the person responsible for this function.

8. Next in the box, write the name of the person currently responsible for this function.

9. No one box should have more than five boxes under it. (In rare cases, no more than seven.)

10. There should be a job description for every horizontal box.

11. There should be policies and procedures for every horizontal group of boxes and for every vertical group of boxes as well as for the organization as a whole.

Do Not Chart
Too Much on One Sheet

Some people try to show every detail broken down on one sheet. They get so much on the sheet that it looks cluttered. It becomes hard to see the relationships of all the individual boxes. An unclear organization chart is about as helpful as not having an organization chart at all. Don't try to put too much on one chart.

First show the organization-wide structure on one chart. This typically includes one box at the top that represents the primary position and function that is being charted. If the function and or position is president or CEO, it is the largest box in place at the top of the sheet. Most of the time sheets are laid out in landscape mode.

Underneath this box, there would be a horizontal row of boxes representing the functions and or positions that report to the president. Under each of those horizontal boxes would be functions and or positions listed vertically that report to those boxes.

To show more detail of the chart, take each box from the horizontal line of the main chart and chart it the same way you did the primary chart. This allows for more detail as the chart goes deeper.

Balance in the Organization

An organization is never as even as it appears on the chart. Charting an organization accurately is more a work of science. Nonetheless, some of the work bundles will be out of balance. They are out of balance because of people. This is where the art part of leadership comes into play.

Some people are naturally more aggressive than others, which leads them to want to dominate in a corporate setting. The leader manager needs to know how to direct them and to hold them accountable. Other people are more passive and tend to get steamrolled. The leader manager needs to know how to help them and hold them accountable as well.

Because people are people, charts can't always depict the organization picture with complete accuracy. However, that does not mean the organization chart is not of value. It is incredibly valuable if you realize that not all of the "people facts" show in the chart.

CHAPTER 14

THE LEADER AND DELEGATION

Getting Work Done through Others

If management is getting work done through others, how does the leader manger do this? The answer is *delegation*.

Some leader managers simply will not delegate. They are afraid that they will lose control. Others delegate but then worry and wonder how much damage subordinates could do if they made a mistake.

The truth is that any person can delegate well if he or she use the technique of the "loose rein." Under this concept, the leader manager delegates fully but keeps a "safety line" in hand.

I experienced the value of the "loose rein" technique firsthand while elk hunting in the mountains of Colorado. I was riding a large, powerful horse while descending a moderate mountain slope. I noticed the horse getting jittery and uneasy. All of sudden it reared its head and took off at full speed. Fear gripped me because we were headed downhill, and I thought the horse might trip and roll with me on it.

I was taught how to ride horses being raised in Texas. I had the reins held loosely in my left hand, as I'm left handed. When the horse began to run, I pulled back with my left hand and then grabbed the reins with my right hand. Now I have both arms pulling back on the reins. The horse finally came to a stop, and I and the horse were uninjured.

In an organization, the essence of the "loose rein" technique is knowledge. A leader manger's knowledge should be of what needs to be happening and what is happening in any area of responsibility. If a subordinate is headed for trouble, the leader manager can pull back on the reins.

The safety line is the loose rein. Using a horse's reins, a person can guide a horse to the right or to the left, make the horse stop or go. After some time, the person and the horse become accustomed to each another and begin to work as a team.

As soon as the driver senses the horse isn't going to dump the wagon in the ditch, the driver can let the reins hang loosely. He doesn't set them aside, though. His hands are still on the reins so to quickly take control if the horse heads for trouble. The driver's ability to pull back on the reins at a moment's notice can prevent serious trouble from happening.

If, however, the horse is properly trotting down the road, the driver holds the reins loosely.

What does this mean for you? Are you someone who delegates to subordinates or should delegate? If so, you have three choices:

1. You can delegate with no reins.

2. You can delegate with tight reins.

3. You can delegate with loose reins.

If you try to hold the reins too tightly, you will eventually tire out. You will wear out yourself and your people, just as the driver of the wagon would exhaust himself and his horse if he constantly jerked and pulled on the reins.

People in an organization grow tired of having to run to the leader manager for every decision. This is especially true of people who are proficient themselves. The loose rein idea brings freedom for everyone: freedom from worry, uncertainty, and the possibility of disaster.

You can compare the driver and the horse situation to the job of managing a group of people in any organization. The leader manager does not need to spend the day doing everyone's work. Instead, he or she must delegate. The leader manager must parcel out some of the responsibility to others, selecting people in whom they have confidence.

Systematic Delegation

So, what are the reins a leader manager can use to help steer the organization? The answer goes back to systems.

Systems planning gives you a number of fundamental reins that you need in order to ensure that your organization travels safely down the road and does not land in a ditch. To apply the systems technique:

1. Define in writing the task that you desire to delegate. Have a clear picture in your mind of the exact nature of the job. Know exactly what you want a team member to do and not do. Take the time to write out the definition of the job. Identify clearly the lines of responsibility and the lines of authority. Tell the team member what is allowed and what is not allowed.

2. Select someone you think can do the job. Jesus carefully selected His disciples before delegating any responsibility to them. He wanted to make sure that He had people who could do the job. In Acts 6, the disciples told the Jews to "choose men of a good report, full of the Holy Spirit, and wisdom" to whom they might appoint to the task of serving food. Some people may not have all of the know-how for the job, but if they have the basic qualities, they can be trained to do the job.

3. Review the description of the task with the person you have chosen. Discuss with the individual how this task relates to the other activities within the organization. Clearly communicate the time elements of the job. Set up specific quantity or quality standards so he or she can compare the actual results against expected results or standards. You and the team member should also be able to check the actual costs against the projected costs. That also can be said for the quality and time expectations. Ask if he or she feels qualified to accept the job. If the answer is no, keep looking.

4. Ask the individual to carefully review the job description and bring back their views and understanding of the job in writing in a certain amount of time. By responding in writing, the prospective team member better identifies where any misunderstanding may arise. As the leader manager, use their written response as a tool to help you both get on the same page. Occasionally at this step, a major discrepancy is identified and both parties agree not to proceed. However, if you both agree, then proceed.

5. Formally assign the job or task.

6. Announce to the rest of the team the new team member's role.

7. Arrange for frequent, regular reports. Notice the word *frequent*. You want to keep track of the progress pulse of the job or task. You cannot do so without proper reporting. You need regular written reports at whatever time intervals you deem necessary. The leader manager should provide the categories of information that will be reported. This can be done through some type of reporting software or a predesigned form in Excel or Word. You can find an example at the end of this chapter. The report should include key indicators of routine work and a space for reporting any developmental or innovative work being performed. Remember, most developed positions that are part of a well-defined system will include 70 percent routine work and 30 percent developmental work.

8. Immediately address any gaps in performance or results. If the reports indicate a need, speak to the team member about the gap immediately. The goal is to find a way to bring performance up to standard by working together or redirecting the team member's actions.

The following is a list of reasons why delegation fails:

- The person was not capable.

- The leader manager failed to match the work to the abilities of the person.

- The person selected had a difficult time making a decision.

- The person was not oriented to work relationships with others.

- The leader manager failed to tell the person exactly what was required.

- The leader manager did not spell out the limits of the worker's authority.

- The work should not have been delegated. It was a leader manager job.

- The leader manager didn't trust the decisions of the delegated person.

- The leader manager did not differentiate between dumping and delegating.

- The leader manager failed to hold a loose rein.

The leader manger should develop the reins jointly with the delegated person. Allow the person who is subject to team limitations to impose restrictions on himself or herself. The person will tend to accept them more readily than if the leader manager imposed them. A self-imposed loose rein will not be met with resistance. The self-imposed loose rein will typically motivate the person to perform at the highest potential.

No one person in an organization is a free agent. Each person bears a cooperative responsibility to the other team members as well as to the person to whom he or she reports. Mature leader managers know they must continually strike a balance between the two seemingly opposing requirements of cooperative teamwork and individual initiative.

Control Must Follow Action

Some leader managers try to exercise control *before* an action happens. They think they can prevent troubles or even minor disasters if they constantly stay ahead of things. The problem is that exercising control before action means there's been no delegation.

If this is something you struggle with, try using the loose rein technique instead. Lay the foundation for control by telling your subordinate what you expect. Give each person, or each group, a definite and continuing responsibility.

Now the team member knows the extent and the limits of his or her responsibility. After you have laid the foundation, exercise control *following* action, not before. Control cannot precede action. Why, you ask? You and your subordinate have agreed on a continuing assignment. How can you control a person before any action?

If you have enough confidence to give a person responsibility, let him or her do the job. At least the first phase of a job, the first 10 percent or 20 percent. After completion of one phase of the work, you can then exercise a degree of control if you have knowledge of the results. Are they the results you want? If yes, you have no need to exercise control. If not, then you tighten the reins.

With a firm hold, you can steer your subordinate away from trouble. When the person is doing okay, leave the reins loose but don't drop them. Remain alert. You can never tell when you must jerk back quickly to avoid difficulties, problems, or even disasters.

Action always precedes control.

Think about it in context of driving a car. When you're cruising on the highway, your hands will probably relax around the wheel. But if the car starts to drift to the left, you turn it back to the right direction. You don't jerk right *before* the car drifts. That's not possible. Take control after action, even after a small amount of action, to ensure that you are empowering your subordinate to do the job.

Delegation Benefits

The leader manager who learns to delegate the safe way, using the loose rein technique, discovers many benefits, including:

1.   The work of the organization goes forward. More work gets done because more people are working well. The leader manager has more time for the responsibilities that only he or she can handle.

2.   Morale and esprit de corps go up. When people are involved, they feel part of the organization. When they feel involved, they are more motivated to support the organization. This is especially true if their efforts are appreciated and they see the results of their efforts.

Delegating the safe way develops responsible leader managers. People may not do the job perfectly the first time, but with guidance, training, and words of encouragement from the leader manager, they will become more effective. And with practice, the organization gains self-confident, capable leader managers.

People Turnover

In this mobile society of ours, we must learn to "live with" turnover. People leave organizations for a variety of reasons such as promotions, family, etc. Sometimes key people leave just after they have been trained. You can't do much about people coming and going. People will move, transfer, become ill, change careers, retire, etc. You can't stop that. But you *can* learn to live with turnover gracefully, and with fewer headaches, if you use written documents and good management practices.

Let's go over some specific techniques.

Long-Range Strategic Plan

A long-range strategic plan brings continuity to the work of your organization. People in group roles and team positions are relatively temporary. If your organization is committed to a long-range work plan, the change of individuals will have less effect on the consistent progress of the organization.

A plan tends to give greater continuity to the efforts of all the people within the organization. It does this despite the shifting and changing that we know will occur. With a long-range plan, you can plug people into the plan more easily because it allows them to see what has been accomplished before they came to the organization. It also shows them what still needs to be accomplished—by them! This informative perspective helps them to get a picture of their new role more quickly than if they were only given the short-term perspective.

Organization Charts

In the last chapter, we talked about the organization chart. This chart can quickly inform people how all of the work of the organization is connected. Without a chart, it may take a new person months to figure out who is responsible for what. The chart helps orient new people so they can find their way around quickly. The quicker they are on-boarded to your team, the sooner they start efficiently plugging away. The organization chart makes this process smooth for everyone.

Policy and Procedures Manual

The policy and procedures manual, aka the rule book, helps your new hires or volunteers sit down on their own time and figure out how everything works. They can quickly grasp *what* their section is supposed to do and *how* the team of that section gets their work done in coordinated activity with each other.

A policy-procedures manual can save you hours of explaining what the purpose of the organization is and how team members function with each other. Instead of coming to you for every policy question, they can consult the manual and figure out what needs to be done. Having policies and procedures clearly written down can also help you in liability areas. Just point the new person to the manual to show them that things are set in stone.

The Job Description

A *job description* lists all the skills and responsibilities that a person needs to handle a specific job. Professional human resource offices use the job description to match the requirements of a job with the qualifications of an applicant.

However, as a business owner or senior ministry leader, it is one of the most effective ways to think on paper about the things that need to get done in your organization. In fact, I like to take the time to develop an "enterprise job description" where all of the key activities or general duties are thoughtfully listed. Then write the name of the person or persons who will be responsible for those key activities or general duties. The goal is to identify everything the organization is doing or needs to do in one document. Sometimes a general duty is so large that several people may be assigned to only one. If that is the case, break down that general duty into several smaller duties.

Next, thoughtfully take as few as one or as many as five of the general duties listed on the enterprise job description and assign them to a particular team member's job description. If there are no team members to assign them to, that will tell you that you need to expand your team.

Taking the time to do this exercise at least twice a year will make you more effective in keeping up with your "enterprise capacity" growth requirements. It also eliminates frustration within you and your team.

Be as clear as possible about the general duties team members will be responsible for. Also identify in each team member's job description the specific duties necessary to accomplish each one of the general duties. List the top three to five specific duties that are the most important for accomplishing a general duty.

One key lesson that I learned the hard way—do not recruit people only to yourself; instead, recruit them to the "system," or in this case, to the job description. A well-written job description is an effective training and on-boarding tool.

At the end of this chapter, you will find a basic outline of a good job description. Notice the categories of Duties General and Duties Specific. They are listed toward the end of the job description, and they capture the General Responsibilities (Duties General) someone in that position would be accountable for accomplishing. Then there are Specific Responsibilities (Duties Specific) that a person is required to do (usually for the purpose of accomplishing the General Responsibilities). The purpose of the job description is to clearly spell out *what* a person is required to do.

The Job Outline

On the other hand, a job outline spells out how to accomplish a task necessary to carry out the specific duties. For example, a *job description* may list a specific duty for an administrative assistant to "Enter all new clients into the company's CRM (customer relationship management software)." The *job outline* spells out the steps that the assistant would take to enter the new client into the software system. The new team member can follow the job outline step-by-step.

Notice how different, but equally important, the objectives of the job description and the job outline are. The job description lists the general and specific duties that a person should fulfill, and the job outline details the steps necessary to carry out a specific duty.

The job outline is a great tool for helping you live with personnel turnover. Job outlines are efficient tools for on-boarding new people into their roles in an organization. You can use a job outline to help a person settle into the "work saddle" quickly. Your aim is to get him or her as productive and as quality conscious as the person who just left the job—and to do it fast. The job outline is a simple tool and one you can fashion easily.

Now, a job outline is not a panacea. You cannot just give a new team member the outline and sit back and think all is well. The outline is simply a good tool in the hands of the person who knows how to use it. Take time to walk a new person through the outline and invite questions about it.

Job Outlines Represent Job Sequences

The job outline should contain information that exactly represents the work. The written version of the job outline should accurately reflect all of the work steps. The two should be the same.

All work starts at one point and finishes at another. The journey from the start to the finish point is a *sequence*. Some cycles are short, consisting of only two or three steps. Short-duration job cycles rarely need to be written down. But other job cycles may have fifteen, twenty, or even fifty different steps before the work is complete. When you write a job outline, line up each step in its logical time sequence. If there are deviations, or side tracks, write these in at the proper point. Then make sure to redirect the work back to the main track a little farther down.

When a job outline is written so that it makes a logical sequence of action, it is easy to write and even easier to read and use. Let me be clear: a job outline covers only *one* cycle of work. Many times one person will use more than one job outline. For example, the Sunday school secretary may need one outline for registering new pupils and one for recording attendance. The secretary will need one more for posting what each class offers. These three jobs may make up the total work bundles of that position.

Select the steps of a job outline in much the same way that you select procedure steps. Pick out a logical starting point for each job. Then trace the steps until you have completed all of the processes that logically fit into this one cycle.

Your Current Team Can Assist

So how do you go about getting a set of job descriptions and job outlines started? Chances are you don't know some of the specific duties and steps to accomplish them yourself. This is where the current employee or volunteer comes into play. Ask for help. This person is doing the job cycles every day! He or she might have difficulty expressing the steps, but together you can put it into writing.

Tell the person who is currently in that position what the job outline is—don't forget to distinguish between the job outline and the job description. Explain the exact work cycle that you want to cover. Be sure the cycle has a definitive start and end point. Ask the employee to suggest a title for each job cycle—something that describes it clearly. The work steps need to be in sequence. The write-up should be clear so when instructing a new employee, the new person will understand readily. Ask the current team to write the instructions in the style of:

1.   If [blank], do X.

2.   Then, do Y.

3.   Next, do Z.

Don't expect a perfect first draft. Anything that the current worker jots down helps you. This is the starting point with details that you need to iron out. Now you can construct the outline into its final form.

In a church, you may have several people doing the same work. For example, if your job outline is for ushers, several people will be doing the same thing. Get one usher to outline how the job is accomplished. Then let the other ushers see this written draft. One person might have a better way of doing a particular step. If so, you can incorporate the "one best way" into the job outline. One person provides you with a springboard for your outline. Others can then contribute.

Sit down with all the team. Find out if the job outline covers just one cycle of work. Are the steps sequential? Are exceptions clearly covered? Are any steps missing? What about terminology? Never throw unknown terms at new people! Avoid initials and acronyms (PERT, PO, WOR, etc.) unless you also explain them. These may be familiar to the current employee and to you, but you will reduce the value of your job outline to the new employee if you use them without explanation. If the new person must have materials to do the work in the outline, explain where to get them. Can you pinpoint a specific drawer or cabinet?

Don't fear length. It doesn't matter how long the job outline may be. If the work cycle requires forty-seven definite work steps, so be it. Cover each step. As you write, you may run into a situation where you have some doubt about whether to combine two steps or to write each separately. When in doubt, always write steps separately.

After you have gone through two or three drafts of the job outline, you will be ready to test it on the next new employee or team member. After the test, you'll probably want to revise it once more. In this way, the outline becomes a tool you can depend upon for training new team members.

Have the new team member first read the job outline. Then go through the steps vicariously by watching the coach do the job. Next, under the eye of the instructor, let the team member do the job alone. When the coach is gone, the trainee can use the job outline as a reference when progressing through the cycle the first few times.

CAUTION: Don't expect miracles of a job outline. Even if you have written it carefully, tested it, checked it, and tried it out with new employees, it won't do the job by itself. It is only a tool, and like a hammer or a wrench, it is only effective in the hands of someone who knows how to use it. Never toss a job outline at a new team member without first giving some personal guidance.

Job Outlines Become Work Habits

After new workers have followed the steps in a job outline a number of times, they will no longer look at it. The work will become second nature. When this occurs, the written work steps have become part of the employee's working pattern. By using a job outline, you transfer the best way of working from your plan-on-paper into the new worker's mind. This "one best way" is simply *the* way. Once formed, habits, whether work habits or personal, are hard to break.

This tendency for the worker to absorb the job outline after doing the work a number of times is a strength, a bulwark against deterioration. With the aid of the job outline, the new person soon performs work swiftly and surely. The result? Continuity and minimal interruption in the organization's operations.

Because some tasks are complex, job outlines are not always sufficient. People must be given some personal training for those types of jobs. Reading a job outline starts the training process, and the trainees can use the job outline for reference as they go along. But reading isn't training. It is only the beginning of the training process—the first exposure. Full absorption of the job is still far away.

This is a fact well known by every effective supervisor and or coach. They also know that many trainees can't read with comprehension. Thus, they explain and show the trainee exactly how to do the job.

Next, the trainer has the trainee try it while observing, and they will discuss what the trainee did right and wrong. The trainee then does it again. The essential goal is absorption. By doing the work, the trainee develops new habits. In this way, the trainee really starts to understand the job.

Training Takes Time

Because time is such a precious resource in many organizations and businesses, we often rush training sessions. We rely on "cram sessions" to squeeze information into people. They absorb some know-how—the key word here being only *some*. Studies have shown that trainees lose 90 percent of information imparted in this way. This is because the trainee has no time to really absorb the information.

Effective training requires the trainee to be motivated in the work process itself. But involvement takes time. Don't rush things or expect miracles. Remember there is always a balance in training between absorption and evaporation.

Getting the Most out of Limited Time

Your time available for training will always be limited. Usually it will be less than you'd like to have. Since time constraints are a chronic condition, what can you do about it? The answer is: make a list of the work that you expect the trainee to absorb and master. Put that list in writing.

Then bring the most important job elements to the top of the list. The items at the top of the list are the jobs that are most necessary in successfully doing the work.

New team members *can* learn a few of the simpler techniques as they go along doing the work. Arrange your list so that the least important items are left for such trial-and-error learning. If the job, for example, breaks down into fifteen minor operations, place the eight or nine most crucial operations at the top of the list. Concentrate your limited training time on those. In this way, you'll use the limited amount of time available to get the most training results.

The Training Process

Training a person to do work is a transfer process. It starts with the person who has the job know-how, usually the trainer, passing on knowledge to a team member who needs it. The teacher needs to have a full grasp of how to do the job. You can't teach what you don't know.

The second essential ingredient for successful training is the teacher's ability to transfer knowledge. Many people can do a job themselves but lack the communication abilities to train another person to do it. The trainer must make sure the right people are in charge of training.

The third ingredient in the training process rests entirely upon the trainee and his or her degree of receptivity. The trainee has to want to do well. If the trainee has no interest in doing well on the job or lacks understanding, knowledge, or experience needed to absorb the training, then the best teacher can't succeed in training that person.

To recap, the three ingredients to a successful training process are:

1.   The job know-how of the trainer.

2.   The trainer's ability to transfer that knowledge.

3.   The trainee's personal receptivity.

Select a Trainable Trainee

The trainer and supervisor may know the job well and have mastered the techniques of good training. But the efforts will be wasted on untrainable trainees—and they do exist. The trainee who is apathetic, too good, too smart, too dull, or simply unsuited for the work, is unable to learn how to do the job well. It will make no difference how good the teacher is.

You cannot coach the untrainable trainee. No matter how you try, you cannot get productivity from unteachable people. Unteachable people are those who don't really want to work, don't care whether they succeed or not, have no interest in their work, or lack potential ability. As trainees, such people are not qualified mentally, physically, or psychologically to absorb the training.

Common Mistakes That Hinder Good Training

Let's recap some common mistakes I have seen trainers make:

1. Relying solely on job descriptions and job outlines to transmit job information.

2. Not allowing sufficient time in the training process.

3. Choosing unreceptive trainees.

4. Lack of know-how on the part of the coach.

5. Trainer lacks ability to transfer information.

By avoiding these mistakes, you are starting off strong on the training game.

Some Principles for Staffing an Organization

1. Set objectives.

2. Develop an efficient plan to help you reach those objectives.

3. Identify and define all jobs.

4. Establish personnel requirements.

5. Begin recruiting early.

6. Select the right person for each job.

7. Plan for training and supervision.

8. Plan for job satisfaction and enrichment.

Weekly Report Form

Name:	Date:	Time Period:

Results

Weekly	Monthly	Year to Date
1) Key Indicator 1	1) Key Indicator 1	1) Key Indicator 1
2) Key Indicator 2	2) Key Indicator 2	2) Key Indicator 2
3) Key Indicator 3	3) Key Indicator 3	3) Key Indicator 3
Planned	**Actual**	**Difference**
1. Task	1. Task	1. Task
2. Task	2. Task	2. Task

Indicate Action: Routine

1. Task
2. Task

Indicate Action: Developmental

1. Task
2. Task

Job Description

Name: _____

Title: _____

Qualifications: _____

- List qualifications for the job
- Required skills
- Software/hardware used

Line of Authority: Shall Oversee and be in charge of all responsibilities in Duties General and Duties Specific

Line of Accountability: Shall be accountable to the President/_____.

General Purpose: To assist the _____
in the _____, _____, and _____ that pertains to
_____ (Business Name).

Duties General:

- General duties the employee will complete

Duties Specific:

- Specific Duties under each Duty General
- List each task needed to complete Duty General

ABOUT
THE AUTHOR

AUTHOR BILLY EPPERHART received his M.B.A. from Colorado State University. Describing himself as a serial entrepreneur, Billy has started seven businesses and owned two franchises. As a real estate investor, he simultaneously owned investment properties in five different states.

Currently, Billy directs two nonprofit companies and is co-director of the Business School of Charis Bible College and serves on the board of Andrew Wommack Ministries. He and his wife, Becky, make their home in Colorado. For more information or to enjoy his weekly financial blog, visit www.billyepperhart.com.

The Harrison House Vision

Proclaiming the truth and the power

of the Gospel of Jesus Christ with excellence.

Challenging Christians

to live victoriously,

grow spiritually,

know God intimately.

Connect with us on
f Facebook @ HarrisonHousePublishers
and ◉ Instagram @ HarrisonHousePublishing
so you can stay up to date with news
about our books and our authors.

Visit us at **www.harrisonhouse.com**
for a complete product listing as well as
monthly specials for wholesale distribution.